YOU ARE ROYALTY
A CHILD OF GOD

Miriam Igeria

YOU ARE ROYALTY – A CHILD OF GOD

Copyright © 2015 Miriam Igeria

Published by:

P.O. Box 58411,
Raleigh, NC 27658
U.S.A.
info@integritypublishers.org

ISBN 978-1-937455-27-9

Publishing Consultants:

Nairobi, Kenya
info@publishing-institute.org
www.publishing-institute.org

All rights reserved. No portion of this book may be reproduced or transmitted in any form or by any means without the written permission of the author or the publisher.

Unless otherwise indicated, Scripture quotations are taken from the HOLY BIBLE, NEW INTERNATIONAL VERSION®. NIV®. Copyright© 1973, 1978, 1984 by Biblica Inc. Used by permission of Zondervan. All rights reserved.

Miriam Igeria has written a very personal testimony to her faith in Christ, which will be an aid to both new and longtime believers alike. Her writing grows out of a deeply held faith that she herself is a much beloved child of God, and that salvation is God's gift (amazing grace), not something we can ever earn. Miriam has a compelling desire to share this good news with all who will hear. In that service she echoes the words of Apostle Paul: "For what I received I passed onto you as of first importance..." The only thing more convincing than Miriam's words is watching her live this faith out in her daily life.

Rev. Peter Moore
Greenfield Presbyterian Church
Berkley, Michigan

Miriam Igeria bears fruit to the honor of God in her latest publication: *You Are Royalty - A Child of God*. As a follower of Jesus, she has always sought faithfulness through a commitment to bring others into a full comprehension of their identity in Christ. Miriam is a leader within the Christian community of metropolitan Detroit, and beyond to the followers in her native Kenya. She ministers with distinction - giving counsel and comfort to the sick of mind, body and spirit. *You Are Royalty - A Child of God* will no doubt introduce her to a broader audience who will find her profound message in a clear and concise manner, and be encouraged to live out their lives as sons and daughters of God.

Kevin Johnson, Pastor
Calvary Presbyterian Church
Greenview, Detroit, USA

Miriam has deep faith in God; she's a lady who is on fire for Jesus. She is undoubtedly proud to be royalty, a princess in the Palace of God, Our Heavenly Father, the King of Kings and Lord of Lords, by virtue of having believed with her heart that God raised Jesus from the dead and confessed with her mouth that Jesus is Lord (Romans 10:9, 10). She is happy and joyful to be a child of God and passionate to share with others about her special relationship with God through His Son Jesus Christ. She is loving and caring and her life is a powerful witness to the reality of God. People are often drawn to her and to the God she is so passionate about and worships with a clear conscience. It is my hope and prayer that her book, "*You Are Royalty – A Child of God,*" will serve as a light for revealing the grace of God in our dark time characterized by self-centeredness, godlessness, enmity, and disobedience against God, Our Creator and Redeemer. Hopefully, it will help those who are in deep crisis and despair, those who feel discouraged and antagonized, realize that they are royalty, children of the Eternal King, and hence cause them to make an about turn and follow Jesus, Our Victorious Savior. May God use the book to help us develop true self-concept, that we're indeed God's most precious children, so that we can learn to have true relationship with Him and one another, behave well, and show love and respect to others, regardless of whether they are our friends or foes.

Rev. Johnson N. Kamau,
Lancaster, Pennsylvania, USA

Contents

Acknowledgements 7
Dedication 9
Foreword 11
Introduction 13
Preface 17

Part 1: Becoming a Child of God 21

Becoming a Child of God 23
Who We Are And Whose We Are 33

Part 2: Growing as Royalty 43

Growing In Royalty 45
Power For The Child of God 57

Part 3: Living as Royalty 63

Fear Not 65
Love 71

Forgiveness	77
Physical Health	83
Joy	87
Family	91
Work	95
Anger	101
Be Prepared For Royalty Problems	103
At Last	107
Bibliography	113

Acknowledgements

I praise God for having guided my life and allowing me to be mentored and taught by some of His best servants. My mother, Loise Wamaitha Kibuka, taught me that hard work never killed anybody along with her favorite verse from Galatians 6:9, *"Let us not become weary in doing good, for at the proper time we will reap a harvest if we do not give up."* My late father, Harun Kibuka taught us to always stand by the truth no matter what happens. One of his favorite verses was Psalm 37:25, *"I was young and now I am old, yet I have never seen the righteous forsaken or their children begging bread."* They also taught us to love each other unconditionally and to practice forgiveness.

I thank my spiritual teachers at PCEA St. Andrew's Church, the Most Rev. John Gatu, the Most Rev. George Wanjau, Rev. Charles Kibicho, Rev. Dr. Timothy Njoya, Rev. Johnson Mwara, Rev. Edward Buri, Rev. Isaiah Muita, Rev. Njenga Kariuki, Rev. Isaac Wanyoike , Rev. Gerishom Kirika who trained me as an assistant hospital chaplain, Rev. Ananie Nduwamungu, Rev. Phyllis Byrd Ochillo, and Rev. Peter Moore of Greenfield Presbyterian Church. The PCEA St. Andrew's Woman's Guild taught me how to serve God's people. The late Mr. Railton Wambugu taught us many life lessons while singing in the choir. Thanks also to Dianne Cragg, choir director of Greenfield Presbyterian church who gave me an opportunity to serve the Lord by praising Him under her direction. When I cannot remember the Bible verses to quote, I easily remember hymns sung many times, e.g., "The Lord is my Light and my Salvation, whom shall I fear." (Psalm 27:1). My other spiritual teachers were the lecturers at the then NIST, now called ILU, and my spiritual teachers at Bible Study Fellowship both in Nairobi and at Bloomfield Baptist Church, Michigan, USA.

Last, but certainly not least, all my siblings and children, especially my brother, Dr. D.K. Gikonyo, who cares for my health and has taught me a lot about staying fit. My other brother, Dr. Gethaiga Kibuka and my sister Veronicah Kibuka read the draft manuscript and encouraged me to write for new believers. My sister-in-love, Dr. B.M. Gikonyo encouraged me to write by saying, "You need to write your story, and everybody has a story to write about their lives." My story begins by thanking God who has protected and guided me. Without Him, I can do nothing. My prayer is from Psalm 138:8, *'the LORD will fulfill [His purpose] for me; your love, O LORD, endures forever-- do not abandon the works of your hands."*

There are many other people who have been a blessing to me and especially in my spiritual life, but I cannot list them all here. God knows them and my prayer is that He would bless them abundantly.

Dedication

To my mother, Loise Kibuka, my children, grandchildren and all believers, especially new ones.

FOREWORD

You are Royalty is a book that comes right from Miriam Igeria's heart. The book is an invitation for the readers to understand, taste and commit to the God who has totally revolutionized Miriam's life. This invitation is an expression of Christian generosity – where we are not faith-holders but faith-sharers. The content expresses that it is possible to live a joyful and impactful Christian life. The chapters demonstrate and guide how to attain that good life.

The book weaves personal experiences, Biblical citations and theological themes, which also reflects the author's personal philosophy in life. Miriam utilizes Biblical wisdom as her practical tool for engaging her life experiences and as a result enjoys the output of great testimonies.

Part one of the book explains how one starts out on the journey of the Christian faith. This is important because many people have questions and seek clarifications on how to begin a journey with Christ as the sole Shepherd.

Upon starting the journey, it is God's will that we grow in obedience and in character. Part two of *You are Royalty* inspires the beauty of Godly progress. It proposes practical ways that will lead to forward movement as well as depth in the Christian faith.

The third part names and expounds on some qualities that are important to invest in so as live a fruitful life in Christ. It also offers guidance on key areas of life – health, family and work.

The book is useful to persons who are seeking to understand the Christian faith. It is also valuable in increasing the understanding of practicing Christians in a way that leads them to fine-tuning their walk with God for an increasingly richer life in Christ. For Christian ministry, it has very accessible and useful content for discipleship.

Pastor Edward Buri,
St. Andrew's Presbyterian Church,
Nairobi, Kenya.

Introduction

I am God's Child.
I am Christ's Friend.
I have been Justified.
I have been Bought with a Price.
I Belong to God.
I am a Member of Christ's Body.
I have been Adopted as God's Child.
I have Direct Access to God through the Holy Spirit.
I have been Forgiven of All my Sins.
I am Complete in Chirst.
I Am GOD's BELOVED CHILD.

This book is written to help new believers as well as those who have been saved for a long time. Through this book I hope to encourage new believers who may be like I used to be before the Lord taught me what it really meant to be born again. I had not internalized what had happened to me and kept on living a defeated life despite knowing that I was born again and in the Kingdom of God.

Jesus said in John 8:31-32, *"To the Jews who had believed Him, Jesus said, 'If you hold to my teaching, you are really my disciples. Then you will know the truth, and the truth will set you free.'"* Becoming Jesus' disciple enables us to know the truth which sets us free.

Some of the truths that set me free include:
1) I am a child of God. John 1:12-13 says, *"Yet to all who received Him, to those who believed in His name, He gave the right to become children of God- children born not of natural descent, nor of human decision or a husband's will, but born of God."*
2) Salvation is free. We are saved by grace through faith in God, not works. Works cannot save anyone.
3) I have eternal life.
4) My sins past, present and future are all forgiven.
5) I am a very important person (V.I.P.) because Jesus died for me.
6) God loves me unconditionally and there is nothing I can ever do to make Him stop loving me, make Him love me more, or make Him love me less.

Once we recognize and internalize these truths we will be free and will glorify God in our lives, because Christ lives in us, guiding us and enabling us to do God's will. Without Him, we can do nothing. The devil is a liar and tries to pull us back to the life we used to live before we were born again. We resist him by submitting to God and remembering that we are new creatures; the old is gone.

Preface

The Bible, the Word of God is the truth communicated to all believers by the loving Father God and it includes many promises made to all who become His children. Becoming a child of God is easy and simple. The way to live as His child is exemplified by the life of Jesus Christ, the Son of God. Some people refuse to be born again into the kingdom of God. Others are born again, but fail to follow Jesus' example thus living defeated lives. All believers who live by faith and not by sight have the ability to live as children of our loving Father. They lead victorious lives despite problems. They know how to submit to God and resist the devil. They live the abundant life that Jesus Christ came to give to all who believe in Him. They rejoice always as commanded by God. They love one another. They make disciples as Jesus commissioned them before He went to heaven. They are able to do all this because God lives in them. The power of the Holy Spirit which enters a believer's heart enables us to do even what the world believes is impossible.

Despite all the promises in the Bible, many Christians live defeated lives because of fear and wanting to follow the crowd. They do not realize that each of us is unique and that God has a specific purpose for each one. That is why

He has given different gifts to believers. As 1 Corinthians 12:7-11 says,

> Now to each one the manifestation of the Spirit is given for the common good. To one there is given through the Spirit a message of wisdom, to another a message of knowledge by means of the same Spirit, to another faith by the same Spirit, to another gifts of healing by that one Spirit, to another miraculous powers, to another prophecy, to another distinguishing between spirits, to another speaking in different kinds of tongues, and to still another the interpretation of tongues. All these are the work of one and the same Spirit, and He distributes them to each one, just as He determines.

It is important to know our gift and use it well for the glory of God. We should not pretend to have all the gifts or to have none. Nor should we compare ourselves with others because we are unique and God has a unique purpose for each of us.

Conforming believers fear persecution although Jesus said they would be persecuted just as He was persecuted. They fear being looked upon as different. They compromise and become weak Christians who are the target of the evil one. They are neither hot nor cold.

The Bible teaches how to live a victorious life as a child of God despite persecution and problems. No matter what people say about us, we continue loving God and following the narrow path of righteousness. It has all the answers to life problems. Once we know the One who walks beside us, we will certainly succeed and continue living as royalty here on earth while awaiting Jesus' return.

Philippians 4:13 --- "I can do all things through Christ who strengthens me."

The Lord has blessed me so much and I want to bless others by sharing what He has been teaching me for many years. I would like to save others from making the same mistakes I made. One of my greatest mistakes was failing to remember who I am and to whom I belong while not forgiving myself for past mistakes. I failed to live as a child of God and enjoy the abundant life that Jesus came to give, glorifying God in all I do. God, in His mercy, has forgiven me all my past sins and I have claimed this abundant life, and live freely as a new and forgiven person. It is said that you should learn from the mistakes of others because you cannot live long enough to make all of them yourself. By sharing my experiences I hope that others will be blessed and become a blessing.

Part 1: Becoming a Child of God

Chapter 1

Becoming a Child of God

Jesus calls people to become children of God in many ways. There are those who are called instantly, like Saul when the Lord appeared to him in Acts 9:1-31. Others hear a sermon preached and when the altar call is made, they accept Jesus Christ as their Lord and Savior. Others are led to the Lord after a prayer meeting or even after meeting a committed believer for the first time. Once God has chosen us, He will use any method in His power to show us His love and mercy until we respond. I am one of those for whom it was a long process because I had the spiritual pride of thinking that I was okay since I was born to Christian parents and baptized as an infant according to Presbyterian Church beliefs. I thought I knew everything and did not want anybody to tell me that I needed to be born again.

As an adult, I realized that born again believers like my mother had something I was missing. I lacked the patience, wisdom and joy that she had. I was easily angered and slow to forgive those who wronged me. I started asking God to help me. I read the New Testament a chapter a day hoping to find salvation. I did not find it. I believed that you cannot be saved while you are in this world but will be saved when you die and go to heaven. Telling people that you are saved while in this world was like saying you have passed an examination before you have taken the test. While here we will continue sinning, so we try to do good works while hoping to be saved in the end. I was very wrong. I did not know that God had provided a solution for all believers who sin because in His wisdom, He knew we could continue sinning, sometimes even unknowingly. 1 John 1:9 says, *"If we confess our sins, He is faithful and just and will forgive us our sins and purify us from all unrighteousness."* It is that simple. Confess, and move on with Jesus holding your hand and telling you, "My child, do not beat yourself, it is all forgiven. Keep on marching on your way to heaven."

It was not until I reached Ephesians 2:8-9 that I allowed the Lord to save me. I was alone in the house reading the New Testament and I learned that, *"it is by grace that we are saved through faith, and this is not by works, it is a gift of God lest anybody should boast."* I learned that salvation is free. It is by grace alone, not by works. I repented of my sins and asked the Lord to forgive me. All my sins, past, present and future were forgiven. That same day I went to a fellowship and gave a testimony of how the Lord had mercy on me and saved me and made me His child.

Although I was eager to help others come to the Lord, I failed miserably. Although I shared my testimony and told people how good God was, I did not succeed in bringing even one person to the Lord. I hated myself for this, forgetting that I am not the Savior. I do not have the power to save anybody or to accuse anybody of sin. The Holy Spirit convicts sinners of their sins; they repent and Jesus saves them. God answered my prayer and desire to lead people to Him when I went to NIST (Nairobi International School of Theology) in

2001 to study Biblical Counseling. I learned an easier way of leading people to the Lord following a small booklet by Bill Bright entitled, "The Four Spiritual Laws". Since then, I have been able to lead several people to the Lord. Still I cannot boast of my power, but the work of the Holy Spirit guiding me.

We become God's children by being born again as Jesus told Nicodemus in John 3:5-8,

> Jesus answered, "Very truly I tell you, no one can enter the kingdom of God unless they are born of water and the Spirit. Flesh gives birth to flesh, but the Spirit gives birth to spirit. You should not be surprised at my saying, 'You must be born again.' The wind blows wherever it pleases. You hear its sound, but you cannot tell where it comes from or where it is going. So it is with everyone born of the Spirit."

The first of the '4 Spiritual Laws' according to Bill Bright says that **God loves you and offers a wonderful plan for your life.** John 3:16 says, "For God so loved the world that He gave His one and only Son, that whoever believes in Him shall not perish but have eternal life." We live a life free of fear of death because we know that God has already given us eternal life as His children. God is eternal and so are His children. In addition to God loving us, God's offer for a wonderful plan for our life is found in John 10:10, "The thief comes only to steal and kill and destroy; I have come that they may have life, and have it to the full." We do not just exist, but live an abundant life. While other people who are not believers may not be enjoying life, we enjoy it because we know who owns us. We know we belong to a Mighty King who is the giver of all good things. We do what is right because He leads us in the paths of righteousness, and we take up our cross and follow Jesus daily and cheerfully.

When Adam sinned, he became separated from God. All Adam's children are separated from God unless they are born again into His Kingdom.

The second Spiritual Law says that **man is sinful and separated from God, thus he cannot know and experience God's love and plan for his life.** He attributes all the good that comes to his life as his own achievement, and when bad things happen to him, he says God is causing his problems. He is always complaining and never content with what God has given him. When God, in His mercy, gives him good health, wealth, and family, he glorifies himself instead of glorifying God. Some use their strength to kill and fight others. Others use their knowledge to spread the word that there is no God. Humans were created to be friends with God. But we chose our own way and friendship with God was broken. This is what the Bible calls sin. This is shown when people rebel against God, do not care about Him and do not live up to His perfect standard. Regarding our sinfulness, Romans 3:10 says, *"There is no one righteous, not even one,* and Romans 3:23 adds, *"For all have sinned and fall short of the glory of God."* Once we realize that we are sinful, we turn to Jesus who is the Only One who can wash away our sins by His blood. There is nothing we can do for ourselves, and there is no earthly person who can help us. We turn to Jesus and ask Him to forgive us. He is faithful and forgives.

The third law says that **Jesus Christ is God's provision for man's sin. Through Him you can know and experience God's love and plan for your life.** He is the only way we can reach God. He died for us. Through Him, we can know and experience God's love and plan for our life. All who believe in Him have eternal life, and when their life on earth ends, they go to live with Jesus in the place He has prepared for believers. 1 Peter 3:18 says, *"For Christ also suffered once for sins, the righteous for the unrighteous, to bring you to God. He was put to death in the body but made alive in the Spirit."*

1 Corinthians 15:3-6 says,

> *For what I received I passed on to you as of first importance: that Christ died for our sins according to the Scriptures, that He was buried, that He was raised on the third day according to the Scriptures, and that He appeared to Cephas, and then to the twelve. After that, He appeared to more than five hundred of the brothers and sisters at the same time, most of whom are still living, though some have fallen asleep.*

God bridged the separation between us and Himself by sending His Son to die on the cross in our place.

Knowing all the above is not enough. The fourth spiritual law according to Bill Bright says that **we must individually receive Jesus Christ as Savior and Lord; then we can know and experience God's love and plan for our lives.** We must be born again as Jesus told Nicodemus. We must receive Jesus Christ as Lord and Savior through faith. As John 1:12-13 says, *"Yet to all who did receive Him, to those who believed in His name, He gave the right to become children of God, children born not of natural descent, nor of human decision or a husband's will, but born of God."* Once we receive Christ in our hearts, we are born into the family of God. Salvation is freely given. We cannot earn it by works. All we need to do is to believe in the Lord Jesus and receive this precious gift by faith.

Rejoice, and again I say rejoice. Once we have made this confession, we are born again and saved. There is no condemnation for us. We are children of God - princes or princesses, and therefore, royalty. From now on we will be referred to as royalty. We will never be alone anymore because we invited Jesus into our hearts. Revelation 3:20 says, *"Here I am! I stand at the door and knock. If anyone hears My voice and opens the door, I will come in and eat with that person, and they with Me."* When we admit that we are sinners and repent, Jesus forgives all our past, present, and future sins. He enters in our purified hearts as He cannot live in sinful hearts. Our bodies are His temple and He will help us to make it strong, healthy and fit to serve Him and others.

The moment that we received Jesus Christ in our heart, many things happened:

1) Christ came into our life. Colossians 1:27 says, *"To them God has chosen to make known among the Gentiles the glorious riches of this mystery, which is Christ in you, the hope of glory."*
2) Our sins were forgiven. Colossians 2:13 says, *"When you were dead in your sins and in the uncircumcision of your flesh, God made you alive with Christ. He forgave us all our sins."*
3) We became children of God. Romans 8:16 says, *"Now if we are children, then we are heirs—heirs of God and co-heirs with Christ, if indeed we share in His sufferings in order that we may also share in His glory."*
4) We received eternal life. John 5:24 says, *"Very truly I tell you, whoever hears my word and believes Him who sent me has eternal life and will not be judged but has crossed over from death to life."*
5) We began to experience God's love and plan for our life. 2 Corinthians 5:17 says, *"Therefore, if anyone is in Christ, the new creation has come: The old has gone, the new is here!"*

Receiving Christ is the best thing that can happen to us. Now that we are princes or princesses, we can dress and groom ourselves and have a nice photo taken as new creatures. We then put this picture in a place where we will be seeing ourselves as royalty every day. We are no longer the same. Our house is now a palace where we live with God the Father, Jesus Christ His Son, and the Holy Spirit. His angels are our bodyguards who protect us day and night. Other believers become our brothers and sisters and we all belong to one Father in the Great Kingdom of love of the Almighty King. We love one another as commanded in God's Word.

Spiritual pride

As new believers we find ourselves on fire. We are excited and ready to do all we can to live this abundant life and witness for Christ. Sometimes new believers can contract a kind of spiritual pride and start persecuting non-believers by forcing them to believe and putting the fear of hell in them. Remember that we are saved by grace. It is a gift of God not of works. We were chosen by God. We were not saved to condemn others, but to tell them the Good News. We cannot save anyone no matter how much we try. That is the work of God alone. The Holy Spirit convicts sinners of their sins, they repent and are saved. Jesus never condemned anyone. He came to seek and save the lost. In the story of the woman who was caught in adultery we see that a crowd gathered wanting to stone her to death but Jesus said in John 8:7, *"Let any one of you who is without sin be the first to throw a stone at her."* All the people left one by one and only Jesus was left with the woman. Jesus told her to go and sin no more. Instead of acting out of pride, James 4:10 says, *"Humble yourselves before the Lord, and He will lift you up"*.

Time

Let's make the best use of the time God has given us. Let's avoid being in a hurry and know that time is one of God's best gifts. We can protect ourselves from suffering from time poverty which causes people to live in a hurry. When we feel we never have enough time, it causes our hearts to beat faster, which can lead to chronic diseases such as diabetes, insomnia, fatigue and high blood pressure. When we know that our time is in God's hands, we can relax and do what He has given us at His pace. Do not fall in the devil's hurry trap. Someone once wrote, *"Are you always too busy? Having no time for yourself, family, God? BUSY = Being Under Satan's Yoke."* So we must be careful how we do our daily chores and glorify God in them. We take every hour of the day and night as an unspeakably perfect miracle.

Dr. John C. Maxwell writes the following about time:

> *How you spend the time that is your own will greatly determine what you think about. No doubt about it – Satan brings his greatest temptations to people when they have time on their hands. It takes discipline of character and proper goals to handle correctly the extra hours given to an individual in our society.*

We can use the free time God gives us to be with friends of good character, read good books, exercise or whatever else makes us happy and helps us become the kind of persons God wants us to be.

Things can go wrong when we are in a hurry. It is said that hurry, hurry has no blessings. We can even end up in accidents simply because we are in a hurry to reach our destination. Slowing down has benefits and God does not want His children to lead a hurried life. My prayer daily is that

God would slow me down so that I can enjoy every second He has given me. It is not a good testimony to non-believers when we are always hurried. They wonder if this is how the God we believe in wants us to live. Their conclusion is that they would rather be the way they are than follow a God who keeps us on the run all the time.

The following hymn by John Newton speaks to the truth of God's amazing grace:

1) *Amazing grace! How sweet the sound*
   That saved a wretch like me!
   I once was lost, but now am found;
   Was blind, but now I see

2) *'Twas grace that taught my heart to fear,*
   And grace my fears relieved;
   How precious did that grace appear
   The hour I first believed!

3) *Through many dangers, toils and snares,*
   I have already come;
   'Tis grace hath brought me safe thus far,
   And grace will lead me home.

4) *The Lord has promised good to me,*
   His Word my hope secures;
   He will my Shield and Portion be,
   As long as life endures.

5) *When we've been there ten thousand years,*
   Bright shining as the sun,
   We've no less days to sing God's praise
   Than when we'd first begun.

Before God in His mercy saved me, I was truly blind. I used to sing the above hymn without understanding. After singing, someone would ask me after leaving the church, "Are you saved?" Believe it or not, I didn't know whether to answer yes or no. I would soon forget that I was singing how amazing this grace is that saved a wretch like me. I would also sing very loudly in church, *"We have heard a joyful sound, Jesus saves! Spread the gladness all around, Jesus saves!"* Still if you asked me if I were saved, I would hesitate to answer, "Yes".

Praise God that I now know I am born again in the Kingdom of God, my Father. I memorized the words from Ephesians 2:8-9 as a reminder that I was saved by grace and nothing else. Salvation is freely given and doesn't depend on my working hard to earn it. Now I do not mock God by singing one thing and living the opposite. I have the assurance of salvation. My sins, past, present and future are all forgiven, and I know I am an heir of eternal life. I also know that I am living in this world and can be tempted to sin. If I sin, I quickly remember the words in 1 John 1:9 of how faithful God is to forgive when we confess.

Chapter 2

Who We Are And Whose We Are

God, our Father wants us to remember always who we are and who we belong to. Aristotle said that we are what we repeatedly do and that excellence is not an act, but a habit. This is very important because the roaring lion wants us to forget and in that moment he attacks. Above all, choose to be happy and to rejoice in the Lord always. Every morning when we wake up, we can affirm who we are and whose we are and we will remain so the whole day. Somebody once said that what we steadily, consciously, habitually think we are, is what we tend to become.

Stephen R. Covey, in his book, "The Seven Habits of Highly Effective People", defines 'habit' as the intersection of knowledge, skill, and desire. He says that our character is a composite of our habits. "Sow a thought, reap an action; sow an action, reap a habit; sow a habit, reap a character, sow a character, reap a destiny," the maxim goes. Habits are powerful factors in our lives. Because they are consistent, often unconscious patterns, they constantly express our character and produce our effectiveness... or ineffectiveness.

Every day as we practice what we know is good and what we want to become, we will grow towards success. We cannot expect to be perfect or take a shortcut. It takes time and must be done one step at a time. Confucius said that a journey of a thousand miles begins with a single step. If we learn and practice the habits mentioned below, we will be amazed by the results.

1. **Habit of loving.** Jesus summed up the 10 commandments into two. *Love the Lord your God with all your heart, with all your soul and with all your mind, and love others as you love yourself.* (Mark 12:30-31). Love the unlovable and our enemies, too, as commanded by God.

2. **Habit of peace.** Remember that when we put our cares into God's hands, He puts His peace into our hearts. Philippians 4:6-7 says, *"Do not be anxious about anything, but in every situation, by prayer and petition, with thanksgiving, present your requests to God. And the peace of God, which transcends all understanding, will guard your hearts and your minds in Christ Jesus."* We want to make it a habit to not be anxious about anything and do all we can to get rid of anxiety. 1 Peter 5:7 says, *"Cast all your anxiety on Him because He cares for you."* Worrying will not help us and may even give us ulcers.

When Jesus told His disciples not to worry in Matthew 6:25-34, He said,

> *"Therefore I tell you, do not worry about your life, what you will eat or drink; or about your body, what you will wear. Is not life more than food, and the body more than clothes?* [26] *Look at the birds of the air; they do not sow or reap or store away in barns, and yet your heavenly Father*

feeds them. Are you not much more valuable than they? ²⁷ Can any one of you by worrying add a single hour to your life? ²⁸ "And why do you worry about clothes? See how the flowers of the field grow. They do not labor or spin. ²⁹ Yet I tell you that not even Solomon in all his splendor was dressed like one of these. ³⁰ If that is how God clothes the grass of the field, which is here today and tomorrow is thrown into the fire, will He not much more clothe you—you of little faith? ³¹ So do not worry, saying, 'What shall we eat?' or 'What shall we drink?' or 'What shall we wear?' ³² For the pagans run after all these things, and your heavenly Father knows that you need them. ³³ But seek first His kingdom and His righteousness, and all these things will be given to you as well. ³⁴ Therefore do not worry about tomorrow, for tomorrow will worry about itself. Each day has enough trouble of its own."

We have to trust and believe Jesus when He tells us not to worry because He cares for us. Once we are in His kingdom, we will never lack anything.

While making peace a habit, it might be useful to memorize the following prayer by St. Francis of Assisi:

Lord, make me an instrument of Your peace.
Where there is hatred, let me sow love.
Where there is injury, pardon,
Where there is doubt, faith,
Where there is despair, hope,
Where there is darkness, light,
and where there is sadness, joy.
O Divine Master, grant that I may not so much seek to be consoled, as to console;
To be understood, as to understand;
To be loved, as to love;

For it is in giving that we receive---
It is in pardoning that we are pardoned;
and it is in dying that we are born to eternal life.

3. **Habit of reading and studying God's Word.** Read the Word of God daily to overcome the devil's temptations. Hide His Word in your heart. When the devil tempted Jesus to turn stones into bread, He told him in Matthew 4:4, *"It is written: 'Man shall not live on bread alone, but on every word that comes from the mouth of God.'"* God promises those who read His Word that He will grant them what they desire, John 15:7, *"If you remain in Me and My words remain in you, ask whatever you wish, and it will be done for you."* The Word of God will also protect us from sinning as written in Psalm 119:11, *"I have hidden your word in my heart that I might not sin against you."* As children of God, there is no way we can grow without reading His Word. We want to feed our soul daily just as we feed our bodies in order to stay spiritually nourished and strong.

4. **Habit of praying:** First thing when we wake up we can thank God for the new day and continue talking to Him throughout the day. Form a habit of praying constantly as is written in 1 Thessalonians 5:17. Jesus commanded His disciples to watch and pray so that they would not fall into temptation. God, our Father likes to hear our voice thanking Him, asking Him for what you need, and interceding for others. Talk to Him frequently throughout the day.

5. **Habit of gratitude:** Form the habit of gratitude. God is pleased when we thank Him. Thank Him for your life which is a special gift from God. We thank Him for the air we breathe. Think of the people who cannot breathe on their own and have to buy oxygen to stay alive. Pray for them. Thank God for saving you and making you His

child. Thank and praise God always and your life will be changed. 1 Thessalonians 5:18 says, *"Give thanks in all circumstances; for this is God's will for you in Christ Jesus."* Please note that we give thanks 'in' all circumstances, not 'for' all circumstances. We give thanks in both good and bad circumstances because God says in Romans 8:28, *"And we know that in all things God works for the good of those who love Him, who have been called according to His purpose."* No matter what is happening, we wait upon the Lord to work everything for our good. Psalm 118:1 says, *"Give thanks to the Lord, for He is good; His love endures forever."* Indeed give Him thanks because He is good and His love for you endures forever.

6. **Habit of praise:** This is a habit we will truly enjoy especially if we love singing. Being part of a church choir can be a blessing but we do not have to be in the choir to praise God. We can praise God anywhere we feel comfortable even if we do not feel we have a great voice. The voice God gave us is the best to make a joyful noise to Him. As we keep on praising Him we will see His wonders. Psalm 150:1-6 is a good example of praise:

[1] *Praise the Lord. Praise God in His sanctuary; praise Him in His mighty heavens.*

[2] *Praise Him for His acts of power; praise Him for His surpassing greatness.*

[3] *Praise Him with the sounding of the trumpet, praise Him with the harp and lyre,*

[4] *Praise Him with timbrel and dancing, praise Him with the strings and pipe,*

[5] *Praise Him with the clash of cymbals, praise Him with resounding cymbals.*

[6] *Let everything that has breath praise the L*ord*. Praise the L*ord*.*

7. **Habit of forgiveness**: Every night when we say our evening prayers, we should remember to forgive anybody who may have wronged us during the day. We also need to forgive ourselves, too. As we confess our sins of commission and omission, God will forgive us as He promised in 1 John 1:9-10, *"If we confess our sins, He is faithful and just and will forgive us our sins and purify us from all unrighteousness. If we claim we have not sinned, we make Him out to be a liar and His word is not in us."* Forgiveness gives peace of mind and prevents diseases which are caused by an unforgiving heart.

8. **Habit of serving:** There is great joy in serving others. If we want to be happy in life, we must learn to serve others because as we serve them, we serve God too. We can visit the sick, prisoners, the needy, the aged and find work to do in the house of God. There is always something to do; we can be a deacon/deaconess, an elder, join/lead a prayer group, join/lead a Bible study, teach Sunday School, care for the homeless, join/lead choir or a praise team.

9. **Habit of trusting God:** *"Trust in the Lord with all your heart and lean not on your own understanding; in all your ways submit to Him, and He will make your paths straight."* (Proverbs 3:5-6). We are too small to lean on our own understanding. Trust in the Almighty God and we will accomplish great things for Him. Like the psalmist we can say, *"I lift up my eyes to the mountains—where does my help come from? My help comes from the Lord, the Maker of heaven and earth"* (Psalm 121:1-2). Also Jesus said in John 15:5, *"Apart from me you can do nothing."*

10. **Habit of practicing your faith:** Hebrews 11:6 says that it is impossible to please God without faith. A believer knows that God can make a way where there is no way, and can

open closed doors as He did when He opened prison doors for Paul and Silas. We can live confidently each day knowing that God will fight battles for us and all we need to do is trust Him.

11. **Habit of thinking positively:** Philippians 4:8-9 says,

> *"Finally, brothers and sisters, whatever is true, whatever is noble, whatever is right, whatever is pure, whatever is lovely, whatever is admirable—if anything is excellent or praiseworthy—think about such things. Whatever you have learned or received or heard from me, or seen in me—put it into practice. And the God of peace will be with you."*

We can ask ourselves if what we are thinking is true, noble, right, pure, lovely, admirable, excellent or praiseworthy. If none of these apply, then our thinking can be harmful to us and others. Somebody once said that if we have good thoughts, they will shine out of our face like sunbeams and we will always look lovely.

12. **Habit of living without fear:** Psalm 118:6-7 says, *'The Lord is with me; I will not be afraid. What can mere mortals do to me? The Lord is with me; He is my Helper. I look in triumph on my enemies."* The Lord has promised to be with us always. We should not be afraid of anything, even of our enemies. Like God helped David triumph over Goliath, He can fight giants in our life. Have courage and let God take away our fear. Psalm 56:3-4 says, *"When I am afraid, I put my trust in you. In God, whose word I praise—in God I trust and am not afraid. What can mere mortals do to me?"* Some people can be afraid at night and cannot fall asleep. God's Word in Proverbs 3:24-26 says, *"When you lie down, you will not be afraid; when you lie down, your sleep will be sweet. Have no fear of sudden disaster or of the ruin that overtakes the wicked, for*

the Lord will be at your side and will keep your foot from being snared." When people are afraid of terrorism, tornadoes, fires, earthquakes, we have confidence in God that He is our refuge. He will protect us.

13. **Habit of listening and talking right:** James 1:19-20 says, *"Everyone should be quick to listen, slow to speak and slow to become angry, because human anger does not produce the righteousness that God desires."* It is very important to listen not only to what others are saying, but to what God is telling us. We must be careful how we answer and how we talk to other people. Proverbs 15:1-2 says, *"A gentle answer turns away wrath, but a harsh word stirs up anger. The tongue of the wise adorns knowledge, but the mouth of the fool gushes folly."* When somebody is angry at us, if we answer softly, it can turn away the anger. The way we talk can show if we are wise or foolish. Choose your words wisely. Proverbs 15:4 also says, *"The soothing tongue is a tree of life, but a perverse tongue crushes the spirit."* As we practice speaking tenderly to others we will reap the sweet fruits of our tongue. Proverbs 13:2-3 says, *"From the fruit of their lips people enjoy good things, but the unfaithful have an appetite for violence. Those who guard their lips preserve their lives, but those who speak rashly will come to ruin."* Learning how to talk well can prolong our lives because we will not provoke the anger of others.

14. **Habit of using time wisely:** It has been said that "Time is money." However, someone else said that time is not money because time is priceless. We can learn to spend our time wisely. If we spend our life doing useless things, we will not fulfill the purpose that God has for us here on earth. Read good books, starting with the Bible, watch good movies that will improve your character. Choose friends who will build you up, not pull you down. Use

time wisely and make the most out of it. Psalm 90:12 says, *"Teach us to number our days that we may gain a heart of wisdom."* We are not going to live forever so must live each day as if it is our last. We also want to avoid wasting other people's time by being late when they need us. Punctuality is critical in our work and elsewhere, such as doctors' appointments and invitations with friends. Redeem time as Ephesians 5:15 cautions, *" Be very careful, then, how you live—not as unwise but as wise, making the most of every opportunity, because the days are evil."*

If we have a procrastination habit, we need to get rid of it. It steals our time. People who plan their time seem to have enough. It is a most precious present. Let's not put off for tomorrow what we can do today and learn to plan in order to help save time. We can make a list of what to do daily, if possible before we go to bed so that when we wake up in the morning, we already know what we have to do. It is often helpful to start with the most difficult thing we feel like avoiding.

There are many habits we need to form as children of God. Psychologists say that if we practice something for twenty-one days, it becomes a habit. With God's help and our persistence we will succeed. Even if we fail from time to time we only need to start again until we succeed and we will be proud of what we will become after our hard work. We can make a mental picture of how we would like to look as royalty. Die to self, take our cross and follow Christ daily. He will help us to lead a victorious life, glorifying God in all we do. Our God is a God who gives second chances and more. God's children are not quitters; they are more than conquerors and we should not lose hope of becoming what God wants us to become. Never let discouragement defeat you or discourage others.

Part 2:
Growing as Royalty

Chapter 3

Growing In Royalty

Pray

As believers, we should joyfully and gratefully anticipate each day. We claim the promise of abundant life and feel energetic. We accept with thanks our "present" from God each day, which is 24 hours = 1,440 minutes = 86,400 seconds. We must not waste even a second of our "present" but should spend it doing what we know will glorify God, our Father. Jesus set an example of waking up early and praying (Mark 1:35), *"Very early in the morning, while it was still dark, Jesus got up, left the house and went off to a solitary place, where He prayed."* It is good to start our day with prayer thanking our Father for the new day and asking Him what He wants us to do for Him. Luke 11:1 tells us that one day when Jesus was praying at a certain place one of His disciples asked Him to teach them to pray. Jesus then taught them the Lord's Prayer. He also taught them to be persistent in prayer. In Luke 11:5-8, a man was awakened and responded to his persistent neighbor who needed food for his guests. Colossians 4:2 tells us to devote ourselves to prayer while being watchful and thankful.

Even though we are grown-ups, our spirits are like those of newborn babies. Our spirits cry to be fed, to be kept warm and it gets thirsty. That is why we need to cry to God in prayer every day. And if we happen to wake up at night and are unable to fall asleep, God is there to listen to us as well. Psalm 34:15 says, *"The eyes of the Lord are on the righteous, and his ears are attentive to their cry."* Tell Him everything, including your secrets. He will keep your secrets and will never laugh at you. Ask Him to guide you throughout the day. We can be confident that nothing will happen during the day that we and God the Father cannot overcome. As we focus on Him the whole day, He will not fail us. We continually pray - some call this, P.U.S.H. (Pray Until Something Happens). Pray for others, our family, our friends, the sick, the needy, the government, pastors and even for those who hate us. Matthew 5:44 says, *"But I tell you, love your enemies and pray for those who persecute you."* Praying is talking to God and also listening and waiting for His answers. Some people pray only when they are in trouble or having problems but we can thank Him and also pray for others. It has been said that prayer is not a "spare wheel" that we pull out when in trouble but rather a "steering wheel" that directs us in the right path throughout life. We need God in both good and bad times and He is with us always. He enjoys hearing our voices talking to Him and He listens.

1 Thessalonians 5: 16-18 says, *Rejoice always, pray continually, give thanks in all circumstances; for this is God's will for you in Christ Jesus."* We cannot pray continually if we only wait until we go to church on Sunday to pray. Praying continually means that we can pray anywhere at anytime. There is no excuse for not praying. We can pray standing up, kneeling down, flat on the ground, walking, jogging, in the bathroom, or driving. God is with us wherever we go and is always ready to listen to our prayers.

Jesus continuously prayed to God the Father and taught His disciples how to pray. In the garden of Gethsemane, Jesus prayed until His sweat was like drops of blood. He told His disciples in Matthew 26:41, *"Watch and pray so that you will not fall into temptation."* Before His ministry, He prayed and taught His disciples how to watch and pray. If Jesus, the Son of God prayed without ceasing, and continues to intercede for us while sitting at the right hand of God the Father, we, as His followers should pray even more. Matthew 7:7-8 talks of A.S.K. which means Ask, Seek, Knock. *"Ask and it will be given to you; seek and you will find; knock and the door will be opened to you. For everyone who asks receives; the one who seeks finds; and to the one who knocks, the door will be opened."* In prayer, we ask God to give us what we need, then keep on seeking until we find it, and lastly, keep on knocking until the doors are opened. Our persistence in prayer does not tire God.

James 1:5-8 talks about asking God for what we need. He gives an example of asking for wisdom which we all need, *"If any of you lacks wisdom, you should ask God, who gives generously to all without finding fault, and it will be given to you. But when you ask, you must believe and not doubt, because the one who doubts is like a wave of the sea, blown and tossed by the wind. That person should not expect to receive anything from the Lord. Such a person is double-minded and unstable in all they do."* Jesus also said in John 14:13-14, *" And I will do whatever you ask in my name, so that the Father may be glorified in the Son. You may ask me for anything in my name, and I will do it."* And again in John 15:7, *"If you remain in me and my words remain in you, ask whatever you wish, and it will be done for you."* Be encouraged to ask. Even when demons asked Jesus not to destroy them, He listened and answered. Mark 5:12-13 says, *"The demons begged Jesus, 'Send us among the pigs; allow us to go into them.' He gave them permission, and the impure spirits came out and went into the pigs. The herd, about two thousand in number, rushed down the steep bank into the lake and were drowned."* If Jesus chose to grant the demons' request, how much more will He answer the prayers of His children? We can ask for what we want with confidence that we will get it as long as it is in His will and is the best for us. In Matthew 7:9-11, Jesus said, *"Which of you, if your son asks for bread, will give him a stone? Or if he asks for a fish, will give him a snake? If you, then, though you are evil, know how to give good gifts to your children, how much more will your Father in heaven give good gifts to those who ask him!"* Although our heavenly Father knows what we need even before we ask, He delights in hearing our voice asking Him for it. If we have a family, we pray with them too. It is said that a family that prays together stays together. Prayer is also like a 'Thank You' note to God. If we have nothing else to tell God, we can always thank Him.

In Ephesians 6:19, Paul says, *"And pray in the Spirit on all occasions with all kinds of prayers and requests. With this in mind, be alert and always keep on praying for all the Lord's people."* Again, praying on all occasions is repeated. If we do not know how to pray, the Holy Spirit is a Teacher. Romans 8:26-27 says, *"In the same way, the Spirit helps us in our weakness. We do not know what we ought to pray for, but the Spirit Himself intercedes for us through wordless groans. And He who searches our hearts knows the mind of the Spirit, because the Spirit intercedes for God's people in accordance with the will of God."*

Some believers like singing and repeating the words in a hymn or Psalm, others meditate quietly using Bible verses which communicate to God how they feel. Praising God chases the demons away and can give great joy to us when singing. Paul and Silas sang and praised God even while in prison. Acts 16: 25-31 says,

"About midnight Paul and Silas were praying and singing hymns to God, and the other prisoners were listening to them. Suddenly

there was such a violent earthquake that the foundations of the prison were shaken. At once all the prison doors flew open, and everyone's chains came loose. The jailer woke up, and when he saw the prison doors open, he drew his sword and was about to kill himself because he thought the prisoners had escaped. But Paul shouted, "Don't harm yourself! We are all here!" The jailer called for lights, rushed in and fell trembling before Paul and Silas. He then brought them out and asked, "Sirs, what must I do to be saved?" They replied, "Believe in the Lord Jesus, and you will be saved—you and your household."

Singing and praying shook the foundations of the prison. Our problems too will be shaken and burdens will fall away as we praise God. The walls of Jericho fell after the priests blew trumpets and shouted as commanded by God. Praising God, shouting and using musical instruments is a great way to please God and watch for miracles to happen. Walls that have been preventing us from getting what we want will fall. As we keep on praising God we will see His wonders. Those who like singing may sing hymns like the ones below about prayer:

1. What a Friend we have in Jesus,
   All our sins and griefs to bear!
   What a privilege to carry
   Everything to God in prayer!
   O what peace we often forfeit,
   O what needless pain we bear,
   All because we do not carry
   Everything to God in prayer.

2. Have we trials and temptations?
   Is there trouble anywhere?
   We should never be discouraged;
   Take it to the Lord in prayer.
   Can we find a friend so faithful
   Who will all our sorrows share?
   Jesus knows our every weakness;
   Take it to the Lord in prayer.

3. Are we weak and heavy laden,
   Cumbered with a load of care?
   Precious Savior, still our refuge,
   Take it to the Lord in prayer.
   Do your friends despise, forsake you?
   Take it to the Lord in prayer!
   In His arms He'll take and shield you;
   You will find a solace there. **Or**

1. Sweet hour of prayer! sweet hour of prayer!
   That calls me from a world of care,
   And bids me at my Father's throne
   Make all my wants and wishes known.
   In seasons of distress and grief,
   My soul has often found relief,
   And oft escaped the tempter's snare,
   By thy return, sweet hour of prayer!

2. Sweet hour of prayer! sweet hour of prayer!
   The joys I feel, the bliss I share,
   Of those whose anxious spirits burn
   With strong desires for thy return!
   With such I hasten to the place
   Where God my Savior shows His face,
   And gladly take my station there,
   And wait for thee, sweet hour of prayer!

3. Sweet hour of prayer! sweet hour of prayer!
   Thy wings shall my petition bear
   To Him whose truth and faithfulness
   Engage the waiting soul to bless.
   And since He bids me seek His face,
   Believe His Word and trust His grace,
   I'll cast on Him my every care,
   And wait for thee, sweet hour of prayer!

4. Sweet hour of prayer! sweet hour of prayer!
   May I thy consolation share,
   Till, from Mount Pisgah's lofty height,
   I view my home and take my flight.
   This robe of flesh I'll drop, and rise
   To seize the everlasting prize,
   And shout, while passing through the air,
   "Farewell, farewell, sweet hour of prayer!"

In addition to prayer, we need to read the Word of God. Reading the Bible is the only way we can know what God wants us to do to glorify Him. In 2 Timothy 3:16-17, Paul said to Timothy, *"All Scripture is God-breathed and is useful for teaching, rebuking, correcting and training in righteousness, so that the servant of God may be thoroughly equipped for every good work."* We no longer do whatever we wish. We may choose where we want to read, however, it is widely accepted that new believers will benefit from beginning in the Gospel of John written by Jesus' beloved disciple. Learning about Jesus' life on earth will change us. It is good to find a plan for reading the whole Bible from Genesis to Revelation. When we combine prayer and Bible reading we will grow and mature in our walk with God. Remember Psalm 119:105 says, *"Your word is a lamp for my feet, and a light on my path."* If you do not have a Bible, you can ask a brother or a sister who has a couple to lend you one while waiting to buy your own. If you have a computer, tablet or smart phone, you can read the Bible online. Do whatever is needed to get your own Bible. The Word of God is referred to as the sword of the Spirit in Ephesians 10:17, *"Take the helmet of salvation and the sword of the Spirit, which is the word of God."* We are now soldiers in the army of God and we need to put on our full armor as directed in Ephesians 6:10-20.

When we read the Bible, we also need to remember to practice what we learn. If we do not put into action what we have read, it is as though we never read the Bible. Our actions speak louder than words and should show non-believers that we are children of God - changed people. We have put off the old and put on the new. James 2:26 says, *"As the body without the spirit is dead, so faith without deeds is dead."* Practice the Golden Rule in Matthew 7:12 until it becomes second nature. *"So in everything, do to others what you would have them do to you, for this sums up the Law and the Prophets."*

It is important to read the Bible as often as possible. Every time we read we learn something new that God wants to teach us. If we say that we have read a certain chapter or verse several times and there is nothing new to learn, we are deceiving ourselves and missing a lot. Just recently, I learned something new from a story I have been reading and hearing about since I was a little girl. It is the story of the man possessed by demons and living in the cemetery. I learned that he was the first missionary to be commissioned by Jesus. *"As Jesus was getting into the boat, the man who had been demon-possessed begged to go with Him. Jesus did not let him, but said, "Go home to your own people and tell them how much the Lord has done for you, and how He has had mercy on you." So the man went away and began to tell in the Decapolis how much Jesus had done for him. And all the people were amazed"* (Mark 5:18-20). If I had not bothered to listen to the preacher thinking that I already knew the story, I would have missed a very important point. Jesus could be telling you the same thing He told the formerly demon-possessed man, *"Go to your own people and tell them how much the Lord has done for you and how He has had mercy on you."* Every believer has something to tell people about what the Lord has done for them. We are all commissioned to tell the Good News.

Go to Church/Fellowship/Bible Study

Just like a newborn baby is cuddled and comforted by parents, relatives and friends, we, too, need the warmth of other believers in order to grow. Other believers are now our brothers and sisters. Fire burns brightly when we add firewood. If we remove one log from the fire and keep it separate, its fire goes out. In the same way, when a believer stays apart from the warmth of other believers, his/her spiritual fire can die. Hebrews 10:24-25 says, *"And let us consider how we may spur one another on toward love and good deeds, not giving up meeting together, as some are in the habit of doing, but encouraging one another—and all the more as you see the Day approaching."* Jesus also encouraged people to pray together. In Matthew 18:19-20, He said, *"Again, truly I tell you that if two of you on earth agree about anything they ask for, it will be done for them by my Father in heaven. For where two or three gather in My name, there am I with them."* If two or three people agree on anything in prayer and God will do it, what about when hundreds or thousands of people are gathered together to pray for peace, the nation, the economy and other things. God will certainly hear what the gathered believers ask for.

Going to church can be compared to taking your car for service after clocking a certain number of miles or kilometers. You do not drive until your car breaks down before taking it in. Once it is taken for service, everything is checked: engine, oil, headlights, parking lights, tyres, wheel balance, and battery. By the time you pick up your car, it is in perfect condition to serve you well for another period of time. In the same manner, your soul needs service. Weekly attendance at church to participate in teaching, prayer and worship helps to keep us going smoothly for the next week until we return. Some people wait until their souls are so malnourished that they need a spiritual ICU to recover.

At the same time, just going to church does not make you a Christian any more than being born in a Christian home does. We go to church because we have become a Christian. We want to have fellowship with our brothers and sisters. Look for a Bible believing congregation where God is worshiped in truth and Spirit. Our brothers and sisters in Christ may guide us to a true church, although no church is perfect since it is made up of imperfect human beings. Follow Christ's teachings, not other people's interpretations. Going to church gives us an opportunity to rejoice with others, thanking and praising God for what He has done. We see and sense God's image and presence in other worshipers. After listening to the sermon, praying and singing, we leave refreshed and energized. As Rev. Peter Moore says, "The worship is over, the service begins."

When we find a church where we want to worship, become a member and begin to serve to continue growing spiritually. Present your tithes and offerings according to how God has blessed you. Visit the sick, the bereaved, the elderly and the needy from your congregation and even those who do not come to your church as long as they need help. Mourn with those who are mourning and rejoice with those who are rejoicing. If you love singing, join the church choir or music ministry. You will celebrate Holy Communion with your brothers and sisters, and if you have not been baptized, you can be baptized along with your family if you so choose. We will always find comfort and company with our brothers and sisters in the church. Remember, though, that the church is not the building. The church that Jesus calls His bride is the group of all those who have a relationship with Him. They could be in any denomination, but they are the church Jesus desires.

The following story, The Silent Sermon, retrieved from Wisdom Commons (http://www.wisdomcommons.org/wisbits/3368-the-silent-sermon) and whose author is unknown may shine a light on why we go to church:

The Silent Sermon

> A member of a certain church, who previously had been attending services regularly, stopped going. After a few weeks, the pastor decided to visit him. It was a chilly evening. The pastor found the man at home alone, sitting before a blazing fire.

Guessing the reason for his pastor's visit, the man welcomed him, led him to a comfortable chair near the fireplace and waited. The pastor made himself at home but said nothing. In the grave silence, he contemplated the dance of the flames around the burning logs.

After some minutes, the pastor took the fire tongs, carefully picked up a brightly burning ember and placed it to one side of the hearth all alone. Then he sat back in his chair, still silent. The host watched all this in quiet contemplation. As the one lone ember's flame flickered and diminished, there was a momentary glow and then its fire was no more.

Soon it was cold and dead. Not a word had been spoken since the initial greeting. The Pastor glanced at his watch and realized it was time to leave. He slowly stood up, picked up the cold, dead ember and placed it back in the middle of the fire. Immediately it began to glow once more with the light and warmth of the burning coals around it.

As the pastor reached the door to leave, his host said with a tear running down his cheek, "Thank you so much for your visit and especially for the fiery sermon. I shall be back in church next Sunday."

Service needs to follow along with our worship. Whatever we do, we serve God. If you are a policeman, you refuse to take bribes and mistreat people. If you are a teacher, you communicate the truth to your students and teach by example. If you are a judge/advocate/lawyer, you serve God by ensuring that justice is done. If you are a farmer, remember that God's children are waiting for your harvest to put food on their table. Do not put harmful chemicals in what you grow.

Chapter 4

Power For The Child Of God

Life isn't meant to be easy,
it's meant to be <u>LIVED</u>.
Sometimes happy,
other times rough...
But within
every up and down
you learn lessons
that make you <u>STRONG</u>.

In Acts 1:8, Jesus told His disciples, *"But you will receive power when the Holy Spirit comes on you; and you will be my witnesses in Jerusalem, and in all Judea and Samaria, and to the ends of the earth."* There is no other way to get power as a child of God except through the Holy Spirit. Early Christians received this power so they could perform great miracles and they did not fear dying for the truth. They were persecuted, but they did not stop sharing the Good News as commissioned by Jesus.

When we are born again, the Holy Spirit enters our heart and we are not the same. We feel the urge to tell others what the Lord has done for us. We are encouraged to share our testimony of how Jesus chose us as His followers, not because we were good, but because He had mercy on us. The power we have will amaze friends and foes.

In a teaching by Bill Bright on "How You Can Be Filled with the Holy Spirit", a man shared this testimony after being filled with the Holy Spirit, "Today I have been liberated!" This man was on the board of twelve Christian organizations. He exclaimed, "I have been trying to serve God so diligently that I practically ignored my business and my family. I have been trying to serve God in the energy of the flesh. I understand now why I have been so miserable and so unproductive!"

After the death of Christ, His disciples were full of fear. They locked themselves in a house praying. Yet these were people who had lived with Jesus for three years and had seen Him perform great miracles. Before Jesus ascended to heaven, He had told them in Acts 1:4-5, *"... He gave them this command: 'Do not leave Jerusalem, but wait for the gift my Father promised, which you have heard me speak about. For John baptized with water, but in a few days you will be baptized with the*

Holy Spirit.'" They obeyed the command and did not leave Jerusalem until they received the Holy Spirit. When Jesus tells us to wait for something, wait for it and it will surely happen. All God's promises are fulfilled, for He does not lie. Numbers 23:19 says, *"God is not human, that he should lie, not a human being, that he should change his mind. Does he speak and then not act? Does he promise and not fulfill?"* God has promised to give us His Holy Spirit. Without Him, we cannot do anything. He is the promised Comforter. He will teach us great things about God. The Holy Spirit is our Governor. His language is unifying. Allow the Holy Spirit to teach us the language of God. We cannot serve God with the energy of our flesh.

In the Word of Faith church in Detroit, U.S.A., a big banner near the altar listed seven steps to spiritual strength:

1. Give Thanksgiving to God
2. Pray in the Spirit
3. Meditate on the Word
4. Confess the Word over Yourself
5. Decide to Walk in Love
6. Be Open to the Holy Spirit
7. Be a Giver. Sow Seed. Give from the Right Motive.

It also listed seven steps to activate God's power:

1. Speak Faith
2. Act Faith
3. Meditate on the Word
4. Practice God's Word
5. Spend Time in Prayer
6. Give Thanksgiving to God
7. Be Obedient to God and His Word

It may seem difficult to practice all the above, but with the help of the Holy Spirit we can do it. He has helped many believers and some have performed many miracles by activating their faith. We can do great things, too, because we believe in an extraordinary God. In John 14:12, Jesus told His disciples, *"I tell you the truth, anyone who has faith in me will do what I have been doing. He will do even greater things than these, because I am going to the Father."*

Just like Jesus, prayed, our prayer and focus should be to do God's will on earth. When God sends us to serve Him, He empowers us by His Holy Spirit. All we need is to obey and follow Him cheerfully. The hymn "Will you come and follow me" has encouraged me a great deal whenever I feel discouraged in my service to God.

WILL YOU COME AND FOLLOW ME

1. Will you come and follow me
   If I but call your name?
   Will you go where you don't know
   And never be the same?
   Will you let my love be shown,
   Will you let my name be known,
   Will you let my life be grown
   In you and you in me?

2. Will you leave yourself behind
   If I but call your name?
   Will you care for cruel and kind
   And never be the same?
   Will you risk the hostile stare
   Should your life attract or scare?
   Will you let me answer pray'r
   In you and you in me?

3. Will you let the blinded see
   If I but call your name?
   Will you set the pris'ners free
   And never be the same?
   Will you kiss the leper clean,
   And do such as this unseen,
   And admit to what I mean
   In you and you in me?

4. Will you love the 'you' you hide
   If I but call your name?
   Will you quell the fear inside
   And never be the same?
   Will you use the faith you've found
   To reshape the world around,
   Through my sight and touch and sound
   In you and you in me?

5. Lord, your summons echoes true
   When you but call my name.
   Let me turn and follow you
   And never be the same.
   In your company I'll go
   Where your love and footsteps show.
   Thus I'll move and live and grow
   In you and you in me.

Part 3:
Living as Royalty

Chapter 5

Fear Not

Because
You are
with me
I will not FEAR
 -Psalm 118:6

God wants us to live without fear. The phrase 'Fear not' is used 365 times in the Bible. God commands us to be courageous in the same way He commanded Joshua in Joshua 1:9, *"Have I not commanded you? Be strong and courageous. Do not be afraid; do not be discouraged, for the Lord your God will be with you wherever you go."* God has promised to be with us wherever we go. He is a Mighty God and when He is with us, nothing can harm us. Once we realize who we are and to whom we belong, fear melts away. God has promised to fight our battles. In Isaiah 41:10, He says, *"So do not fear, for I am with you; do not be dismayed, for I am your God. I will strengthen you and help you; I will uphold you with my righteous right hand."* Even though we may experience fear, we can take courage from God's presence and power in our lives. When other people are trembling with fear as they face situations, which are frightening, we have an inner sense of confidence. Some might even think we are foolish. They might ask us, "Don't you know how the economy has become so bad and people are suffering. Why do these things not frighten you? Haven't you heard how terrorists and gangsters are terrorizing people, and yet you act as if you are not worried?" We will not let our actions be based on fear.

There are times when things might look bleak; David compared it to passing through the dark valley of the shadow of death. Even then, God has commanded us not to fear. He says in Isaiah 43:1-3, *"Do not fear, for I have redeemed you; I have summoned you by name; you are mine. When you pass through the waters, I will be with you; and when you pass through the rivers, they will not sweep over you. When you walk through the fire, you will not be burned; the flames will not set you ablaze. For I am the Lord your God, the Holy One of Israel, your Savior."*

No matter what is happening in our lives, God knows it and He will help us. We will overcome because He who is in us is greater than he who is in the world. He loves us and will not allow anything that is not for our good to happen to us. So even though we may feel fear in such situations, we know that our God is on our side and will carry us through. Fear does not have to dictate our actions.

When Jesus gave the great commission just before He ascended to heaven, He promised His disciples that He would always be with them. We are now His disciples and the promise is ours too. *"Then Jesus came to them and said, "All authority in heaven and on earth has been given to me. Therefore go and make disciples of all nations, baptizing them in the name of the Father and of the Son and of the Holy Spirit, and teaching them to obey everything I have commanded you. And surely I am with you always, to the very end of the age."* Matthew 28:18-20. So, cast away any fear and obey this great commission. Go and make disciples now that you have become one. We have been blessed. Be a blessing to others by telling them of the love of Jesus and what He has done for you.

Erroneous assumptions can also cause fear. The root of all fear is a lack of trust in the Lord. If fear creeps in remember that we are protected and God is our refuge. He is our Shepherd. Psalm 27:1-3 says,

> *[1] The Lord is my light and my salvation— whom shall I fear? The Lord is the stronghold of my life—of whom shall I be afraid? [2] When the wicked advance against me to devour me, it is my enemies and my foes who will stumble and fall. [3] Though an army besiege me, my heart will not fear; though war break out against me, even then I will be confident.*

When others who do not believe in God are failing because of fear, we know our God will never fail us. We walk with confidence wherever we go. God prospers the work of our hands and we have courage to do things that frighten others. We remember who we are and whose we are. We also know what Isaiah 54:17 says, *"No weapon forged against you will prevail, and you will refute every tongue that accuses you. This is the heritage of the servants of the Lord, and this is their vindication from me' declares the Lord."*

Focus on Christ and do not follow the crowd. Trust in God and do what is right. When we are focused on Him, nothing can distract us. Guided by Christ we move on from the life we used to live to reach greater heights. It is not wise to look back when we are enjoying abundant life. There is a lot of work to be done for the Lord. Jesus said the harvest is great, but the laborers are few. We have no time to sit idle. When we think of the work Jesus did in only three years, we are challenged to see what we can achieve with His help.

We have enthusiasm and are not idle. We avoid drugs and alcohol and anything else that would dull our senses. We want to be alert all the time lest Jesus return and find us sleeping. When we see those who have no relationship with Jesus getting drunk, we pray for them. It is sad that without alcohol, some people have no life. We have the Giver of abundant life in us and do not need alcohol. He said in John 14:6, *"I am the way and the truth and the life. No one comes to the Father except through me."* The Spirit of God keeps us high all the time and we do not need stimulants.

We are also wearing the full armor of God as instructed in Ephesians 6:10-17:

> *"Finally, be strong in the Lord and in His mighty power. Put on the full armor of God, so that you can take your stand against the devil's schemes. For our struggle is not*

against flesh and blood, but against the rulers, against the authorities, against the powers of this dark world and against the spiritual forces of evil in the heavenly realms. Therefore put on the full armor of God, so that when the day of evil comes, you may be able to stand your ground, and after you have done everything, to stand. Stand firm then, with the belt of truth buckled around your waist, with the breastplate of righteousness in place, and with your feet fitted with the readiness that comes from the gospel of peace. In addition to all this, take up the shield of faith, with which you can extinguish all the flaming arrows of the evil one. Take the helmet of salvation and the sword of the Spirit, which is the word of God.

When we are fully armed like this, we have no cause to fear. We march on as soldiers of Christ with confidence that we will accomplish the purpose God had for us when He brought us into this world. It has been said that the chief aim of man is to glorify God and to enjoy Him forever.

William P. Young's character Mack in his book, "The Shack" asks God, "So why do I have so much fear in my life?"

God answered, "Because you don't believe. You don't know that We [Trinity] love you. The person who lives by their fears will not find freedom in My love. I am not talking about rational fears regarding legitimate dangers, but imagined fears, and especially the projection of those into the future. To the degree that those fears have a place in your life, you neither believe I am good nor know deep in your heart that I love you. You sing about it; you talk about it, but you don't know it."

Chapter 6

Love

> *"See what great love the Father has lavished on us, that we should be called children of God! And that is what we are! The reason the world does not know us is that it did not know him. Dear friends, now we are children of God, and what we will be has not yet been made known..."*
>
> 1 John 3:1-2

God is love. Now that we are His children, we need to demonstrate this attribute which is in our DNA because God is our Father. Love is the mark of a Christian. We begin by loving God as Jesus taught in Mark 12:30-31, *"Love the Lord your God with all your heart and with all your soul and with all your mind and with all your strength.' The second is this: 'Love your neighbor as yourself.' There is no commandment greater than these."* When we love God as commanded, we will then be able to love others as we love ourselves. We cannot love others without the love of God. We cannot give what we do not have. Ephesians 5:1-2 says, *"Follow God's example, therefore, as dearly loved children and walk in the way of love, just as Christ loved us and gave himself up for us as a fragrant offering and sacrifice to God.*" Learn to love others like Jesus loves us. He loves us as if you are the only ones on earth.

1 John 3:11 says, *"For this is the message you heard from the beginning: We should love one another."* Love others, including your enemies as commanded by God. It is hard to love and pray for our enemies, but we obey because it is a command. Leave it to God to deal with your enemies; He will do it well. Our responsibility is to obey and love them. With the help of the Holy Spirit, we can do that and be assured that God is able to change our enemies. He can also use them to teach us great life lessons which friends might not be able to do. Be motivated by love in everything. Selfishness will melt away and people will respond to the love we show them. We will spread love to others and teach them how to love. We must show love to our families. As a man, you will love your wife as God commanded in Ephesians 5:25-28,

> *"Husbands, love your wives, just as Christ loved the church and gave himself up for her to make her holy, cleansing her by the washing with water through the word, and to present her to himself as a radiant church, without stain or wrinkle or any other blemish, but holy and blameless. In this same way, husbands ought to love their wives as their own bodies. He who loves his wife loves himself."*

Regarding loving our enemies, Rev. Johnson Kamau wrote,

> *"What is real love? Real (or true) love is to love somebody who does not deserve your love at all; it is to go out of your way to show kindness to someone who, humanly speaking, you would rather hate with your whole heart, simply because he or she does not deserve your love at all. That's*

what real love is: loving those who in actuality do not qualify to be loved by you. That is divine love, and it is truly powerful! Please, read 1 John 4:7-11."

One of the ministers at St. Andrew's Church, Rev. Edward Buri, wrote the following about loving our enemies.

> "Love your enemies..." Really? Sounds serious. But seriously, the consumers of the Good Book would find it more palatable if the instruction had a selective option – that way we would love only the loveable enemies.
>
> When the "how-you-did-in-life" award ceremony comes, I predict there will be few crowns in the "enemy huggers" category! Love my enemies? The spirit is wishing but the fangs are itching...with venom. What is this about blasting bombs that grind your lifetime valuables into dust...in seconds? What is there to be polite about those who shred children into orphans? Is it not evil to embrace anyone whose calling is to melt wives into widows and husbands into widowers? Thoughts of loving such heartless lots are a strange luxury afforded only by those with affections to waste.
>
> The Good Book...The Great Good Book insists, "...for if you only love those who love you, how different will you be from others...." Stop. Different? What difference? The only difference that counts is the number of bullets that go into the enemies' chest.
>
> But hard times demand hard ideologies. "Love your enemies..." Let's call this Love-ocracy. Loveocracy is beyond democracy. At the core of loveocracy is the wisdom that the Maker of the Universe would rather see us love-toting than gun-toting. Loveocratization is the key to a new

community – a different community. The driving wisdom of loveocracy is that you do not differentiate yourself from the enemy by becoming an advanced version of the enemy. If we become advanced versions of the enemy, all the enemy needs to overtake us is an upgrade!

Interestingly, Paul of Tarsus gives love a militant edge, "...it is heaping hot coals..." Love has its weapon side, and it is just a matter of time before love melts the enemy – if not in life, in hell."

Love yourself. Every morning when you look at the mirror, affirm yourself and say as it is written in Psalm 139:14, *"I praise you because I am fearfully and wonderfully made; your works are wonderful, I know that full well."* We are made in the image of God. Everything God makes is beautiful. If you feel you have a big mouth, be sure that God did not make a mistake in giving you that mouth. Maybe He wanted you to be a preacher, a politician, a singer where you will enjoy using your big mouth. Find out what His will is for you and how to use your mouth to glorify Him. Love your body whether you are thin or fat, tall or short, black or white. Accept yourself the way your loving God made you. Each of us is unique, special and valuable. God has a special purpose for you and He wants to use you to serve Him, just as you are. You are His masterpiece. As we receive God's love we are more able to love ourselves which is a key factor in emotional health. When we love ourselves as children of God, we are able to see God's image in others and love them as commanded. When we love God first, everything else falls into line, and then we will be able to really love ourselves and do what God wants us to do.

1 Corinthians 13:1-13 says,
If I speak in the tongues of men or of angels, but do not have love, I am only a resounding gong or a clanging cymbal. [2]

If I have the gift of prophecy and can fathom all mysteries and all knowledge, and if I have a faith that can move mountains, but do not have love, I am nothing. ³ If I give all I possess to the poor and give over my body to hardship that I may boast, but do not have love, I gain nothing.

⁴ Love is patient, love is kind. It does not envy, it does not boast, it is not proud. ⁵ It does not dishonor others, it is not self-seeking, it is not easily angered, it keeps no record of wrongs. ⁶ Love does not delight in evil but rejoices with the truth. ⁷ It always protects, always trusts, always hopes, always perseveres. ⁸ Love never fails. But where there are prophecies, they will cease; where there are tongues, they will be stilled; where there is knowledge, it will pass away. ⁹ For we know in part and we prophesy in part, ¹⁰ but when completeness comes, what is in part disappears. ¹¹ When I was a child, I talked like a child, I thought like a child, I reasoned like a child. When I became a man, I put the ways of childhood behind me. ¹² For now we see only a reflection as in a mirror; then we shall see face to face. Now I know in part; then I shall know fully, even as I am fully known. ¹³ And now these three remain: faith, hope and love. But the greatest of these is love."

As we read these words, we realize that without love we are nothing even if we have all the other gifts of the Holy Spirit. Love holds all the others together and is the key to living a godly life.

Jesus told His disciples in John 14:16-17, *"If you love me, keep my commands. And I will ask the Father, and He will give you another advocate to help you and be with you forever— the Spirit of truth."* He also said in verse 23, *"Anyone who loves me will obey my teaching. My Father will love them, and we will come to them and make our home with them."* In John 15: 12-13, Jesus continues to talk about love, *"My command is this: Love each other as I have loved you. Greater love has no one than this: to lay down one's life for one's friends."* 1 John 2:10 also says, *"Anyone who loves their brother and sister lives in the light, and there is nothing in them to make them stumble."*

Every day we need to demonstrate our love for others in word and deed. We seek to help those who are in need, to visit those in prison, or in hospitals and homes. After the verb "love", "help" is the most beautiful verb in the world. We will no longer bear to see a brother or sister in need without being filled with compassion for them. We no longer think only about ourselves and our family but always remember our new family, the family of God, our Father. We are not kind to others expecting anything in return. We do it for love's sake and nothing else.

If we love others, we do not want them to go to hell so we share our testimony by telling what God has done for us, and the great miracle of salvation that Jesus freely gives. We are like beggars telling others where to get the bread we have found. The opposite of love is not hatred, but indifference. Simply tell others what God has done for you. Lead them to the Savior who saved you by grace. They do not have to do anything as salvation is freely given to whoever is willing to receive it by faith.

God hears the cry of a repentant sinner. He will never turn anyone down. Our job is to tell and leave the rest to God.

Chapter 7

Forgiveness

We are aware that we are God's children but it is hard to forget how we were before we were forgiven. Does God keep reminding us of all that we did before He forgave us? No! He forgives, gives us a new heart and starts a clean page in our life. It is said that harboring unforgiveness is like drinking poison hoping your enemy will die. If we do not forgive those who have wronged us, we may suffer from many chronic diseases. Our choice to forgive does not depend on whether the other person repents or not. We will feel better and our emotional health will improve. Learn to forgive yourself, too. If you cannot forgive yourself, it will be difficult to forgive others.

Forgiveness will open us up to receive blessing. We will have peace because we are no longer bothered by what was done to us. Forgiveness does not mean forgetting what was done to us nor does it mean that it was alright. It is for our own good that we move on with our life trusting that God will take care and do justice to whoever wronged us.

In Matthew 18:21-35, there is a story of a man who could not forgive:

> [21] Then Peter came to Jesus and asked, "Lord, how many times shall I forgive my brother or sister who sins against me? Up to seven times?" [22] Jesus answered, "I tell you, not seven times, but seventy-seven times. [23] Therefore, the kingdom of heaven is like a king who wanted to settle accounts with his servants. [24] As he began the settlement, a man who owed him ten thousand bags of gold was brought to him. [25] Since he was not able to pay, the master ordered that he and his wife and his children and all that he had be sold to repay the debt. [26] "At this the servant fell on his knees before him. 'Be patient with me,' he begged, 'and I will pay back everything.' [27] The servant's master took pity on him, canceled the debt and let him go. [28] "But when that servant went out, he found one of his fellow servants who owed him a hundred silver coins. He grabbed him and began to choke him. 'Pay back what you owe me!' he demanded. [29] "His fellow servant fell to his knees and begged him, 'Be patient with me, and I will pay it back.' [30] "But he refused. Instead, he went off and had the man thrown into prison until he could pay the debt. [31] When the other servants saw what had happened, they were outraged and went and told their master everything that had happened. [32] "Then the master called the servant in. 'You wicked servant,' he said, 'I canceled all that debt of yours because you begged me to. [33] Shouldn't you have had mercy on your fellow servant just as I had on you?' [34] In anger his master handed him over to the jailers to be tortured, until he should pay back all he owed. [35] "This is how my heavenly Father will treat each of you unless you forgive your brother or sister from your heart."

Jesus taught His disciples to forgive each other. In the Lord's Prayer, we ask God to forgive our sins as we forgive those who sin against us. In Matthew 6:14-15, Jesus said, *"For if you forgive other people when they sin against you, your heavenly Father will also forgive you. But if you do not forgive others their sins, your Father will not forgive your sins."* Forgiveness is one of the virtues of a Christian. If we find ourselves harboring unforgiveness, we can ask God to help us find the way to let go and heal so that bitterness does not destroy our life and testimony. This is a process and may take time and help from others who can support our desire to forgive.

William P. Young, in "The Shack", writes, *"Forgiveness is first for you, the forgiver, to release you from something that will eat you alive; that will destroy your joy and your ability to love fully and openly."* The person who wronged us may not care how we feel. In fact he or she might be happy to know that we are feeling hurt. Choose to forgive. Release the one who has wronged you to God so that He can deal with them. We may never forget what that person did, but when we release them to God, He deals with them and us in the way He believes is best.

Some people live bitter, unforgiving lives and think of revenge. As children of God, we must work with God's help to move beyond this unhealthy bitterness. Romans 12:19-21 says,

> *"Do not take revenge, my friends, but leave room for God's wrath, for it is written: "It is mine to avenge; I will repay,"* says the Lord. On the contrary: "If your enemy is hungry, feed him; if he is thirsty, give him something to drink. In doing this, you will heap burning coals on his head." Do not be overcome by evil, but overcome evil with good."

GIVE

"For God so loved the world that He gave His one and only Son, that whoever believes in Him shall not perish but have eternal life" (John 3:16).

God is a giver. He gave His only Son so that you and I could have eternal life. He set the example for all believers to be givers. Be generous and give according to how God has blessed you. The Bible says that it is more blessed to give than to receive. Proverbs 22:9 says, *"The generous will themselves be blessed, for they share their food with the poor."* Luke 6:30-31 also says, *"Give to everyone who asks you, and if anyone takes what belongs to you, do not demand it back. Do to others as you would have them do to you."*

When we give, we also receive. This is a law of nature and not only for believers. Jesus commanded His followers to be givers when He said in Luke 6:38, *"Give, and it will be given to you. A good measure, pressed down, shaken together and running over, will be poured into your lap. For with the measure you use, it will be measured to you."* I have seen this in my life as I have received much after giving relatively little. It is also true that the measure we use will be used for us. The measure of prosperity is not how much we have, but how much we give.

Remember to give to your church in the form of tithes and offerings. Our tithe is ten percent of our gross income from our business or salary. An offering would be something we give above and beyond our tithe. When we give, we are not to do so grudgingly. A story was told about a certain man in Nyeri, Kenya. He had travelled from the city and went to church in the rural area where people use pit latrines. He carried a lot of money in his wallet, but he only wanted to offer the smallest bill. When it was near offering time, he went to the latrine so that he could select the smallest bill to give to the church. As he was struggling to get the smallest note from the large bundle of bills, his wallet fell into the pit which was about 30 feet deep. The story goes that he ran out of the latrine shouting, "It has to be demolished! It has to be demolished! It has to be demolished!" Some people from the congregation who heard him shout thought he had gone mad and went to find out what had to be demolished. He then explained how his wallet with a lot of money in it fell in the pit.

Another man from the same area thought he was clever. He went to a nearby shop to change some money before going to church. He put the little money he wanted to offer in one of his coat pockets, and the big bills which he did not want to offer, in another pocket. When the plate was passed, he dipped his hand into his pocket and put the money in. After the service, he realized that he had given the larger bills instead of the small ones and what was left was not even enough for his bus fare. He asked a friend who was with him if it would be okay to go back to church and ask for his money back. His friend told him he should let it be and consider it as the offering he should have been giving to God all the years that he rarely went to church.

2 Corinthians 9:6-7 says, *"Remember this: Whoever sows sparingly will also reap sparingly, and whoever sows generously will also reap generously. Each of you should give what you have decided in your heart to give, not reluctantly or under compulsion, for God loves a cheerful giver."* When we give generously, God will bless us abundantly in a variety of ways, not necessarily with material wealth. He is the one who has given everything to us. In fact, He does not need our money. He just wants to see how grateful we are that He has enabled us to work and receive all that we have. Give so that the church can help those who are sick or those who are poor. If we sow sparingly, we will reap sparingly.

If we do not offer our tithes, we are robbing God. Malachi 3:8-12 says,

> *"Will a mere mortal rob God? Yet you rob me. But you ask, 'How are we robbing you?' In tithes and offerings. ⁹ You are under a curse—your whole nation—because you are robbing me. ¹⁰ Bring the whole tithe into the storehouse, that there may be food in my house. Test me in this,"* says the Lord Almighty, *"and see if I will not throw open the floodgates of heaven and pour out so much blessing that there will not be room enough to store it. ¹¹ I will prevent pests from devouring your crops, and the vines in your fields will not drop their fruit before it is ripe,"* says the Lord Almighty. ¹² *"Then all the nations will call you blessed, for yours will be a delightful land,"* says the Lord Almighty."

God will fulfill His promise to us. If we give our tithes, He will bless us just as He has said. He will open the floodgates of heaven and pour out abundant blessings in many areas of our lives, not just materially or financially. God wants us to test Him in this. My mother was my best example in giving. The more she gave, the more we were blessed. Instead of becoming poorer, she had plenty. When we give what we have, it is like creating room for God to put more into our lives.

Chapter 8

Physical Health

Our body is the temple of the Holy Spirit. In 3 John 1:2, the Bible says, *"Dear friend, I pray that you may enjoy good health and that all may go well with you, even as your soul is getting along well."* As we take care of our health, we will more easily enjoy what He has blessed us with in this world. Good health does not come automatically. We must eat healthy foods, exercise, and rest as well as avoiding alcohol, drugs and cigarettes.

Alcohol and drugs dull our senses. As God's children, we want to be alert to be able to watch and pray. Protect your life and the lives of others by remaining sober in order to be productive for our Lord.

It is also wise to be careful about what we eat so that we do not fill our body with junk and carry unwanted weight. A balanced diet consists of eating fresh fruits and vegetables, proteins and limited carbohydrates, as well as drinking plenty of water. Exercise helps build strong muscles and bones. Soldiers get up early to exercise in order to stay strong to fight and defend the country. We are in God's army and need to be strong both physically and spiritually.

When we are weak, we cannot serve God as well as we would like to.

God has promised His people rest. He gave us six days to work and one day to rest. This is for our own good. If we choose not to rest, our health will suffer. Just as a car needs to be taken in for service to run well, if we overwork our body without rest, it will break down. Seven to eight hours of sleep a night is advisable.

Sometimes we can do our best to stay healthy, yet we still get sick. If this happens, trust God. He knows we are sick and is able to heal us. It could be a trial like what Job went through. The devil wanted him to curse God but he did not, even when he lost everything including his children. Pray for healing as in James 5:14-16, *"Is anyone among you sick? Let them call the elders of the church to pray over them and anoint them with oil in the name of the Lord. And the prayer offered in faith will make the sick person well; the Lord will raise them up. If they have sinned, they will be forgiven."* When Jesus walked on this earth He healed many and even raised the dead; He can still do this today as we ask Him in prayer. Isaiah 53:5 says, *"But He was pierced for our transgressions, He was crushed for our iniquities; the punishment that brought us peace was on Him, and by His wounds we are healed."* Jesus is able to heal us. Remember this verse and how He suffered so that we may be whole both physically and spiritually. Many miracles of divine healing are taking place all over the world today. If it is His will to heal us, there is no sickness too great for Jesus. However, there are times when God uses illness and death to accomplish His purposes in our lives and thus we, or our loved ones will not be healed until reaching perfect wholeness in heaven.

When we feel unwell, it is important to see a doctor. Do not just sit at home praying. God uses doctors who are qualified to treat you according to your diagnosis. Refusing to go and see a doctor is like testing God and is not good. We know God can heal us when we pray but He uses different methods, including doctors and medicine. When Jesus was on earth there were times when He would just say a word, and the person would be healed. Another time He spit on the dirt, made mud and put it on the blind person's eyes and he was able to see again. God is not limited in the means He may choose to use for our benefit. Psalm 103:2-3 says, *"Praise the Lord, my soul, and forget not all his benefits— who forgives all your sins and heals all your diseases."*

When we visit the doctors, they may carry out tests to find out what is causing our sickness. Perhaps we are lacking some nutrients in our body and with supplements our body can heal. Other times, we may need to lose some weight to alleviate various problems. Do not test God like some Christians who say God will heal them even without going to the hospital. It is good to have strong faith, but remember God also uses doctors as His servants to bring about our cure. If we refuse to go to the hospital and die, we cannot blame God for not healing us. We chose not to use a channel of healing that God might have used to heal us.

Chapter 9

Joy

*I can be perfectly
happy with my
life if I do not
expect things to go
PERFECTLY!*

"....The joy of the Lord is your strength" (Nehemiah 8:10). When we are joyful, it makes our spirit and body strong. This will not depend on our circumstances, but on the knowledge that when we have God, we have everything, and He is always on our side. Joy is a choice we make daily. Do not expect others to make you happy. Situations will certainly come and cause us to feel sad or discouraged, but we can choose not to let what is happening deny our joy. One way to be happy is to make someone else happy. When we feel sad, think of others who are not as blessed as we are - those who are sick, or have lost loved ones, or are homeless, or hungry. We will soon start counting our blessings. Start thanking God for what He has given you freely, your life, health, food, spouse, children, shelter, job, and your sadness will melt away. If nothing else makes you happy, rejoice that you are a child of God, and that He has saved you and forgiven all your sins, and now you have eternal life. We are new creatures who have passed from death to life.

Smile to keep your face looking cheerful. A woman who was once asked why she kept on smiling, answered, "Because God is taking my picture." Keep on smiling and avoid an expensive facelift or botox. A smile is an inexpensive way to improve our looks. Above all, it will glorify God to reflect His joy on our faces.

Karl Barth said, *"Joy is the simplest form of gratitude."* We cannot help feeling and expressing joy if we live with an attitude of gratitude. We have a lot to be thankful for. We cannot remain joyless once we start praising God and should not let the mood swings of others determine how we feel. Instead, we can spread joy wherever we go. When life gives us a hundred reasons to cry, we show that we have a thousand reasons to smile.

Proverbs 17:22 says, *"A cheerful heart is good medicine, but a crushed spirit dries up the bones."* It is said that joy is a choice. We can choose to have joy under all circumstances.

If we as Christians are always gloomy, we need to ask ourselves if we are all right. Grimness is not a Christian virtue. If God is the center of our life, we can find joy. If we have no joy, no one will believe the Good News we tell which should make us joyful before we share it with others. Our misery can have serious consequences causing our bodies as well as our souls to suffer.

There is a difference between joy and happiness. Happiness is the result of being pleased with who we are, what we have and what we do. Joy, on the other hand, comes from God and from knowing that the King of kings has chosen us, loved us and forgiven us. We may be old, sick, friendless, poor, blind, halt, and lame. But if we know the Source and Giver of life, we have the gift of joy.

The story, Amazing Advice on Happiness at 92-years Old (author unknown), (http://successify.net/2014/04/10/wisdom-happiness-92-years-old/) provides pointers on how to find happiness:

> *The 92-year-old, petite, well-poised and proud lady, who is fully dressed each morning by eight o'clock, with her hair fashionably coifed and makeup perfectly applied, even though she is legally blind, moved to a nursing home today. Her husband of 70 years recently passed away, making the move necessary.*
>
> *After many hours of waiting patiently in the lobby of the nursing home, she smiled sweetly when told her room was ready. As she maneuvered her walker to the elevator, I provided a visual description of her tiny room, including*

the eyelet sheets that had been hung on her window. "I love it," she stated with the enthusiasm of an eight-year-old having just been presented with a new puppy.

"Mrs. Jones, you haven't seen the room .... just wait."

"That doesn't have anything to do with it," she replied. "Happiness is something you decide on ahead of time. Whether I like my room or not doesn't depend on how the furniture is arranged, it's how I arrange my mind. I already decided to love it. It's a decision I make every morning when I wake up. I have a choice; I can spend the day in bed recounting the difficulty I have with the parts of my body that no longer work, or get out of bed and be thankful for the ones that do. Each day is a gift, and as long as my eyes open I'll focus on the new day and all the happy memories I've stored away, just for this time in my life."

She went on to explain, "Old age is like a bank account, you withdraw from what you've put in. So, my advice to you would be to deposit a lot of happiness in the bank account of memories. Thank you for your part in filling my memory bank. I am still depositing."

And with a smile, she said: "Remember the five simple rules to be happy:

1. Free your heart from hatred.
2. Free your mind from worries.
3. Live simply.
4. Give more.
5. Expect less.

God will show us how to find our own joy. He loves you and wants you to be joyful to glorify Him.

Chapter 10

Family

The first place to practice being a child of God is in the family. If you are married, treat your spouse as commanded by God. The Bible has all the answers on to how to solve conflicts in marriage as well as the hierarchy God intended. If you are a woman, your husband is the head of your family and it is important to submit to him. Before you marry a man in a Christian marriage, ask yourself if he is the right man to head your family. If he cannot lead in the position God has given him, he is not the man for you. A man must be willing to obey God to be able to lead a godly family. If you are a man, check whether your wife to be is willing to submit to you. If not, there will be two heads of one family and it is very confusing. Ephesians 5:21-33 says,

> *Submit to one another out of reverence for Christ. Wives, submit yourselves to your own husbands as you do to the Lord. For the husband is the head of the wife as Christ is the head of the church, his body, of which he is the Savior. Now as the church submits to Christ, so also wives should submit to their husbands in everything.*

> *Husbands, love your wives, just as Christ loved the church and gave himself up for her to make her holy, cleansing her by the washing with water through the word, and to present her to himself as a radiant church, without stain or wrinkle or any other blemish, but holy and blameless. In this same way, husbands ought to love their wives as their own bodies. He who loves his wife loves himself. After all, no one ever hated their own body, but they feed and care for their body, just as Christ does the church— for we are members of his body. "For this reason a man will leave his father and mother and be united to his wife, and the two will become one flesh. This is a profound mystery—but I am talking about Christ and the church. However, each one of you also must love his wife as he loves himself, and the wife must respect her husband.*

Love your family with all your heart. It is good to have friends, relatives, colleagues, but our core family needs first priority in our attention and love. Some people spend more time with their friends or at work than with their families so that the families suffer by missing one of their members. If you are single, you still have a family. Our parents and siblings are our first priority.

Love and honor your parents as the Bible commands. Ephesians 6:1-4 says, *"Children, obey your parents in the Lord, for this is right. "Honor your father and mother"—which is the first commandment with a promise— "so that it may go well with you and that you may enjoy long life on the earth." Fathers, do not exasperate your children; instead, bring them up in the training and instruction of the Lord."*

"Love begins by taking care of the closest ones-the ones at home."
— Mother Teresa of Calcutta

If you are a parent, ask yourself what your children think of you. If they were to write about you, what would they say? Dr. John C. Maxwell wrote this in his book entitled, "Think on These Things."

> *It was from my parents, Melvin and Laura Maxwell that I learned early in this life lesson about thinking right. They are two of the most godly and most positive people I've ever known. In all my years growing up, I never heard them talk negatively about other people. They continually dwell on what is good and live out their beliefs every single day.*

I wonder what my children would say about me. I raised them as a single parent after their father passed away in an accident when they were very young. I put my trust in God and told my children that they had two fathers in heaven. God, our heavenly Father, and their earthly father who went to heaven when he died. Children are better off when raised by two parents, as raising them alone is a very difficult task. Sometimes though that is not possible. I made many mistakes, but since they were His children, I trusted that God would see them through and let His Holy Spirit teach them where I could not. By His grace, I did my best and I believe they turned out all right. None of them gave me sleepless nights by disobeying me. I thank and praise God for them.

With regard to my parents, they taught us to be givers, especially to the needy, charity and the church. They also taught us to always stand by the truth and never to repay evil for evil, but to overcome evil with good. (Romans 12:17-21). My father was a man of very high integrity and used to say that the church begins at home. One cannot go to teach how to lead a godly life in church on Sundays while one lived a hell-like life at his home the rest of the six days. They taught us to walk the talk. My father added that the best business was one which was run by a man and his wife. (*Mbiacara njega no ya mũndũ na mũtumia wake*). They practiced what they preached and we emulated them. They loved all of us equally. They did not have a favorite child and emphasized on educating both girls and boys to the highest level one could get to.

Chapter 11

Work

Whatever we do in the work week is important and we should see it as service to God. Ecclesiastes 9:10 tells us, *"Whatever your hand finds to do, do it with all your might, for in the realm of the dead, where you are going, there is neither working nor planning nor knowledge nor wisdom."* So, we should put all our energy, enthusiasm and joy in whatever God has given us to do to glorify Him. Work is a blessing, not a curse. When God created Adam and Eve, He gave them the work of tending the Garden of Eden. Learn to enjoy the work you do and if you do not like it, change your job or change your attitude. The following hymn may give you some joy as you work.

> 1. *Work, for the night is coming,*
> *Work through the morning hours;*
> *Work while the dew is sparkling,*
> *Work 'mid springing flowers;*
> *Work when the day grows brighter,*
> *Work in the glowing sun;*
> *Work, for the night is coming,*
> *When man's work is done.*

2. *Work, for the night is coming,*
   Work through the sunny noon;
   Fill brightest hours with labor,
   Rest comes sure and soon.
   Give every flying minute,
   Something to keep in store;
   Work, for the night is coming,
   When man works no more.

3. *Work, for the night is coming,*
   Under the sunset skies;
   While their bright tints are glowing,
   Work, for daylight flies.
   Work till the last beam fadeth,
   Fadeth to shine no more;
   Work, while the night is darkening,
   When man's work is o'er.

A time will come when we can no longer work. So, keep on working before the night comes. Let your work glorify God.

Ephesians 5:15-16 says, *"Be very careful, then, how you live—not as unwise but as wise, making the most of every opportunity, because the days are evil."* Be faithful in your work and do it well. Don't work just to please your supervisor but to please God. Ephesians 5: 7-8 says, *"Serve wholeheartedly, as if you were serving the Lord, not people, because you know that the Lord will reward each one for whatever good they do, whether they are slave or free."* Make the best of every opportunity. Report to work on time. When we start our work even five minutes late, we are stealing from our employer because we will be paid for those five minutes just as if we had worked.

We cannot afford to be slothful when Jesus came to give us abundant life. The Bible tells us to be busy serving the Lord. Love for our Master makes us want to spend our time serving

Him well. Wherever we work, we know He is watching. Our employer may underpay us for a job well done, but our Master has better payment. Deuteronomy 2:7 says, *"The Lord your God has blessed you in all the work of your hands. He has watched over your journey through this vast wilderness. These forty years the Lord your God has been with you, and you have not lacked anything."* Like those Israelites, we also will lack nothing and God will continue to bless the work of our hands as long as we live.

Proverbs 10:4-5 says, *"Lazy hands make for poverty, but diligent hands bring wealth. He who gathers crops in summer is a prudent son, but he who sleeps during harvest is a disgraceful son."* Laziness does not glorify God. Proverbs 15:19 says, *"The way of the sluggard is blocked with thorns, but the path of the upright is a highway."* Those who obey God and work hard, move on to greater blessing.

Proverbs 6:6-11 says,

> *"Go to the ant, you sluggard; consider its ways and be wise! ⁷ It has no commander, no overseer or ruler, yet it stores its provisions in summer and gathers its food at harvest. ⁹ How long will you lie there, you sluggard? When will you get up from your sleep? ¹⁰ A little sleep, a little slumber, a little folding of the hands to rest— ¹¹ and poverty will come on you like a thief and scarcity like an armed man."*

Jesus set an example for us to follow. He woke up very early and accomplished much every day. In a period of three years, He achieved more than most people will accomplish in a lifetime. It is said that God feeds the birds of the air, but He does not put food in their nests. They have to wake up early, and after singing praises to God, He shows them where to go and get their food. If they stayed in their nest, they would starve to death.

2 Thessalonians 3:10-13 (The Message) says, *"Don't you remember the rule we had when we lived with you? 'If you don't work, you don't eat."* And now we're getting reports that a bunch of lazy good-for-nothings are taking advantage of you. This must not be tolerated. We command them to get to work immediately—no excuses, no arguments—and earn their own keep. Friends, don't slack off in doing your duty.". When we obey God and do the work He has given us we will have plenty to share with those in need.

Finances

When we work, we get paid but sometimes it seems that no matter how hard we work, there is never enough money. Learn to be content in all circumstances. When we are blessed with much, remember to share with the needy. Hebrews 13:16 tells us not to forget to do good and to share with others, because God is pleased with such sacrifices. When we give to God's people, we are giving to God. It is said that the love of money is the root of all evil. Money itself is not evil but we need to use it wisely and not let it use us. Hebrews 13:5 says, *"Keep your lives free from the love of money and be content with what you have, because God has said, 'Never will I leave you; never will I forsake you.'"* Remember that our prosperity is not measured by how much we have, but how much we give.

No matter whether we have much or little we can keep on seeking and asking God for His blessing. He is our Shepherd and will meet our needs as David said in Psalm 23. Philippians 4:19 says that, *"God will meet all your needs according to the riches of His glory in Christ Jesus."* So keep on asking, seeking and knocking until He opens a door for you to receive what you need. He loves you and there is nothing you can do to make Him love you more or to stop loving you. If God blesses you with wealth, beware of worshiping your property instead of God. All good things come from God and we would have nothing without Him. Let God be God and give Him first place in your heart.

Resting and having fun

God worked six days and rested on the seventh. The fourth commandment in Exodus 20:8-11 says,

> *Remember the Sabbath day by keeping it holy. Six days you shall labor and do all your work, but the seventh day is a Sabbath to the Lord your God. On it you shall not do any work, neither you, nor your son or daughter, nor your male or female servant, nor your animals, nor any foreigner residing in your towns. For in six days the Lord made the heavens and the earth, the sea, and all that is in them, but he rested on the seventh day. Therefore the Lord blessed the Sabbath day and made it holy.*

Because God loves us, He wants us to rest after working hard. He wants us to have time to recover and restore our energy. If we do not obey this commandment, eventually our health will suffer. God knows what our bodies need more than we do. He also wants us to use this Sabbath time to worship Him and to reflect on His goodness.

God also wants us to enjoy life. Take time to have fun in God-pleasing ways. Ecclesiastes 11:9-10 says, *"You who are young, be happy while you are young, and let your heart give you joy in the days of your youth. Follow the ways of your heart and whatever your eyes see, but know that for all these things God will bring you into judgment. So then, banish anxiety from your heart and cast off the troubles of your body."* In Psalm 127:1-2, it is written, *"Unless the Lord builds the house, the builders labor in vain. Unless the Lord watches over the city, the guards stand watch in* vain. *In vain you rise early and stay up late, toiling for food to eat— for He grants sleep to those He loves."* All our work will be in vain if we are not seeking to please God. Let God help you as His child. Our job is to trust and obey Him. He knows what we need even before we ask.

Chapter 12

Anger

The Word of God in Ephesians 4:6 says, *"In your anger do not sin"; do not let the sun go down while you are still angry, and do not give the devil a foothold."* God knows that we will get angry sometimes. Even Jesus got angry when people had made His temple a den of robbers. But in your anger, be careful not to sin. We may be tempted to hate the person who made us angry which can lead us to do evil things to hurt them. When we get angry, we must not let the sun go down when we are still angry. God knows it is difficult for us to sleep well when we are angry. If you and your spouse have a conflict, do your best to resolve it before sleeping.

God has promised to take revenge for us so we can leave it to Him. He can even change the heart of the one who has wronged us to make him/her humble to repent and apologize. Do good to those who hate you and overcome evil by doing good. We will have peace of mind and we will be blessed for obeying God's Word. Colossians 3:8 says, *"But now you must also rid yourselves of all such things as these: anger, rage, malice, slander, and filthy language from your lips."* Every day, when you say your prayers, ask God to help you rid yourself of any of these. The Holy Spirit will guide and enable us to live according to His promises. We cannot do this in our own power.

Proverbs 22:24-25 says, *"Do not make friends with a hot-tempered person, do not associate with one easily angered, or you may learn their ways and get yourself ensnared."* It is very easy to copy our friends' habits. When we associate with people who are short-tempered and easily angered, we may become like them. Ecclesiastes 7:9 says, *"Do not be quickly provoked in your spirit, for anger resides in the lap of fools."*

Chapter 13

Be Prepared For Royalty Problems

There is a hymn by John W. Peterson which says,

1. It's not an easy road we are trav'ling to Heaven,
   For many are the thorns on the way;
   It's not an easy road but the Savior is with us,
   His presence gives us joy ev'ry day.

   > No, no, it's not an easy road,
   > No, no, it's not an easy road.
   > But Jesus walks with me and brightens my journey,
   > And lightens ev'ry heavy load.

2. It's not an easy road, there are trials and troubles,
   And many are the dangers we meet;
   But Jesus guards and keeps so that nothing can harm us,
   And smooths the rugged path for our feet.

3. Tho' I am often footsore and weary from travel,
   Tho' I am often bowed down with care;
   A better day is coming when Home in the glory,
   We'll rest in perfect peace over there.

The journey to heaven will not be easy. The devil gets angry when we leave his kingdom to join God's Kingdom. He will do anything to make us return to him. Be prepared for trials and temptations when they come your way. Always remember, however, that Jesus will carry you through; He will never leave you alone. We will be overcomers and nothing can come our way without Jesus being aware of it. He is our refuge and will protect us. We can call on Him and He will answer us. James 4:7 says, *"Submit yourselves, then, to God. Resist the devil, and he will flee from you."* We submit to the Lord first because we cannot resist the devil without the Lord. Then the Lord will give us strength to resist. After that, we will surely believe that we are more than conquerors as Romans 8:31 says, *"What, then, shall we say in response to these things? If God is for us, who can be against us?"* Romans 8:37 says, *"No, in all these things we are more than conquerors through him who loved us."* Jesus' love for us will never allow the devil to defeat us. Even if he kills us, Jesus will take us to be with Him in heaven. When trials and troubles come our way, as they come to all believers, remember who we are and whose we are. We are royalty, children of our heavenly Father. Jesus knew all this would happen to His disciples and He told them in John 16:33, *"I have told you these things, so that in me you may have peace. In this world you will have trouble. But take heart! I have overcome the world."* Do not be discouraged when troubles come. Be of good cheer because Jesus has told us to take heart. Since He has overcome the world, we will overcome too.

1 Peter 5:8-9 says, *"Be alert and of sober mind. Your enemy the devil prowls around like a roaring lion looking for someone to devour. Resist him, standing firm in the faith, because you know that the family of believers throughout the world is undergoing the same kind of sufferings."* Here the devil is compared to a roaring lion

looking for someone to devour. We can imagine how those who are unprepared for troubles and do not resist the devil are tormented.

James 1:2-4 says, *"Consider it pure joy, my brothers and sisters, whenever you face trials of many kinds, because you know that the testing of your faith produces perseverance. Let perseverance finish its work so that you may be mature and complete, not lacking anything."* Often when I am convicted by a message from a preacher, or when I have read a portion of the Bible teaching me something about the Lord, trials follow. This serves as a reminder that God teaches us before a test to enable us to overcome. The living Word sinks into our heart more deeply during trials than at any other time. Without trials, how will we know if we can overcome? That is why James says that we should consider it pure joy whenever we face trials. We become people of strong character through perseverance.

There are other reasons why we should count it pure joy when we suffer. Romans 5:3-4 says, *"Not only so, but we also glory in our sufferings, because we know that suffering produces perseverance; perseverance, character; and character, hope."* We learn some things only during our darkest times. When the bottom drops down, it is not beyond God's reach. God is able to lift us up and comfort us. He is an expert in mending broken hearts. He changes caterpillars into butterflies, sand into pearls, and coal into diamonds using time and pressure. He is working on us when we are under pressure and hardships.

When we are tempted, or trials come or evil things happen in the world, we should not blame God. He is full of goodness and does not wish any of His children evil. James 1:13-14 says, *"When tempted, no one should say, "God is tempting me." For God cannot be tempted by evil, nor does he tempt anyone;*

but each one is tempted when, by his own evil desire, he is dragged away and enticed."

Jesus himself in Luke 9:23-24 says, "If anyone would come after me, he must deny himself and take up his cross daily and follow me. For whoever wants to save his life will lose it, but whoever loses his life for me will save it."

Chapter 14

At Last

As a child of God, we know that He will never abandon us. We may hear all kinds of stories about what will happen when we die. Some may say we will be asleep in the grave until Jesus' return. Others are of the opinion that we go to heaven or hell the moment we die. Still others reckon that we will never go to heaven because that is a place for the chosen few, i.e., 144,000 saints so the remaining believers will live on the new earth which God will create. We do not need to concern ourselves with where we will be. Our heavenly Father knows where He will take us after we leave this world. Rev. Peter Moore of Greenfield Presbyterian Church says that dying is like sleeping in one room and waking up in the next. He gives an example of an older brother taking his younger brother who has fallen asleep on the couch in the living room to his bed in his bedroom. When the little brother wakes up, he might wonder how he got there since he fell asleep in the living room. In the same manner, we will fall asleep (die) while here on earth, and God will lift us up to where He is, and we will wake in the beautiful place that Jesus has gone to prepare for us.

In John 14:2-4, Jesus said, *"My Father's house has many rooms; if that were not so, would I have told you that I am going there to prepare a place for you? And if I go and prepare a place for you, I will come back and take you to be with Me that you also may be where I am. You know the way to the place where I am going."* We do not need to be troubled. If we believe in Jesus, we know that He went to prepare a place for us, and when it is ready, He will come and take us there. He said that all we need to know is that He is the Way (John 14:6). Our responsibility is to trust and obey while doing God's will here on earth. Matthew 7:21 says that not everyone who says to Him, 'Lord, Lord,' will enter the kingdom of heaven, but only the one who does the will of God who is in heaven. Every day when we wake up, pray that God will show us His will so that we will do what He wants during the day. As His children, we are constantly growing in our ability to demonstrate our love for God and those around us by doing what pleases Him.

Do not judge others

> *"Do not judge, or you too will be judged. For in the same way you judge others, you will be judged, and with the measure you use, it will be measured to you"* (Matthew 7:1-2).

We are on a journey travelling to heaven. As we travel, we should not go alone but tell others about our journey and where we are going so that they too can join us in that place of eternal joy. Avoid spiritual pride and a holier-than-thou attitude. Isaiah 64:6a says that all of us have become like one who is unclean, and all our righteous acts are like filthy rags. God is the only one to judge who is righteous and who is not. Jesus said in Matthew 7:3-5, *"Why do you look at the speck of sawdust in your brother's eye and pay no attention to the* plank in your own eye? How can you say to your brother, 'Let me take the speck out of your eye,' when all the time there is a plank in your own eye? You hypocrite, first take the plank out of your own eye, and then you will see clearly to remove the speck from your brother's eye."* Convicting others of their sins is the work of the Holy Spirit, not ours. The work of saving others belongs to Jesus, not to us. Our job is to share the Good News so that others may hear, believe and be saved. We love them just as they are, although we do not condone sin.

We can use our time to edify others and help them grow in their Christian life. If we are busy judging others, we will not have time to love them. If we gossip about someone, we are wasting our life. If we spend time trying to change others, it keeps us from changing the only person we can truly change, ourselves. If we spend our time improving ourselves then we will have no time to disapprove of others. The only person we need to compare ourselves to is the person we were yesterday.

I used to be very good at judging others. I could find fault with almost everyone. It was like I was the only perfect person sitting on God's judgment seat. I knew which denominations that had lost their way and was sure that their followers would not go to heaven because of this or that. I believed people in my denomination would be the only ones to go to heaven.

God helped me overcome this spiritual pride. He taught me that when Jesus returns, He will not take denominations to heaven. He will take individuals who love and believe in Him irrespective of their denomination. He taught me that all those who have a relationship with Jesus after accepting Him as their Lord and Savior will go to heaven. Believers will go to heaven because of their relationship with God. At the same time, there may be people in every denomination who will go to hell because they do not have a faith relationship with Him. The teachers or preachers in those denominations who mislead the congregation will be punished for misleading God's children.

As mature children of God, we should not let others mislead us. By reading the Bible we will know what God wants. God has given us a brain to think and reason. He has given us His Holy Spirit as our Teacher. As we pray and read God's Word we will know His will and He will help us accomplish our goals for His glory.

When our work on earth is done, we will say like Paul in 2 Timothy 4:7-8, *"I have fought the good fight, I have finished the race, I have kept the faith. Now there is in store for me the crown of righteousness, which the Lord, the righteous Judge, will award to me on that day—and not only to me, but also to all who have longed for his appearing."* We will live with Jesus forever and ever. We will meet all our loved ones who have gone before us. There will be no more pain, no more crying, and no more dying, just praising and rejoicing with the angels in heaven. All believers live with the hope of going to heaven when they die.

I conclude by praising and thanking God with the following hymn:

> 1. *Guide me, O Thou great Jehovah,*
> *Pilgrim through this barren land.*
> *I am weak, but Thou art mighty;*
> *Hold me with Thy powerful hand.*
> *Bread of Heaven, Bread of Heaven,*
> *Feed me till I want no more;*
> *Feed me till I want no more.*

2. Open now the crystal fountain,
   Whence the healing stream doth flow;
   Let the fire and cloudy pillar
   Lead me all my journey through.
   Strong Deliverer, strong Deliverer,
   Be Thou still my Strength and Shield;
   Be Thou still my Strength and Shield.

3. When I tread the verge of Jordan,
   Bid my anxious fears subside;
   Death of deaths, and hell's destruction,
   Land me safe on Canaan's side.
   Songs of praises, songs of praises,
   I will ever give to Thee;
   I will ever give to Thee.

I am the daughter/son of a King,

who is not moved by the world

For my God is with me

and goes before me.

I do not fear because

I am His.

Bibliography

Bright, B. (1991). *How You Can Be Filled With the Holy Spirit.* Nairobi: Life Ministry.

Coghill, A. L. (1854). *Work for the Night is Coming* http://www.cyberhymnal.org/htm/w/o/workfort.htm

Covey, S.R. (1990). *The 7 Habits of Highly Effective People.* New York: Simon & Schuster.

Maxwell, J.C. (1999). *Think on These Things.* Kansas City: Beacon Hill Press.

Newton, J. (1779) *Amazing Grace* http://www.hymnary.org/text/amazing_grace_how_sweet_the_sound

Peterson, J.W. (1952). *It is not an Easy Road* http://www.pine- net.com/~joanbab/itsnot.htm

Scriven, J.M. (1855). *What a Friend we Have in Jesus* http://www.cyberhymnal.org/htm/w/a/f/wafwhij.htm

Walford, W. (1845). *Sweet Hour of Prayer* cyberhymnal.org/htm/s/h/shop.htm

Willims W. (1745). *Guide me O Thou Great Jehovah,* http://www.cyberhymnal.org/htm/g/u/guideme.htm

The Silent Sermon http://scifac.ru.ac.za/cathedral/spire/nov03/sermon.htm

Young, W. P. (2007). *The Shack*. Los Angeles: Windblown Media.

www.ingramcontent.com/pod-product-compliance
Lightning Source LLC
LaVergne TN
LVHW021400080426
835508LV00020B/2369